*Ninety-Nine Names
of the
Beloved*

Ninety-Nine Names of the Beloved

*Intimations
of the Beauty and Power of the Divine*

Camille Hamilton Adams Helminski

First edition published 2017
by Sweet Lady Press,
an imprint of Threshold Books

© Camille Hamilton Adams Helminski, 2017

Hardcover ISBN: 978-0-9981258-1-7
Paperback ISBN: 978-0-9981258-2-4

All rights reserved. No part of this publication may be reproduced or utilized in any form or by any means, electronic or mechanical, including photocopying, or by any information storage and retrieval system, without prior written permission from Sweet Lady Press.

Library of Congress Cataloging-in-Publication Data

Names: Helminski, Camille Adams, 1951- author.
Title: Ninety nine names of the beloved : intimations of the beauty and power of the divine / Camille Hamilton Adams Helminski.
Description: First edition. | Louisville : Sweet Lady Press, 2017.
Identifiers: LCCN 2017028680 | ISBN 9780998125817 (hardcover)
Classification: LCC PS3608.E464 N57 2017 | DDC 811/.6--dc23 LC record available at https://lccn.loc.gov/2017028680

SWEET LADY PRESS
1288 Cherokee Road
Louisville, Kentucky 40204

www.sufism.org

Table of Contents

Preface
ix

Introduction
xv

The Most Beautiful Names

1. *Ar Rahman*, The Infinitely Compassionate 1
2. *Ar Rahim*, The Infinitely Merciful 1
3. *Al Malik*, The Sovereign 4
4. *Al Quddus*, The Most Holy and Pure 8
5. *As Salaam*, The One Who Is Peace 11
6. *Al Mumin*, The Most Faithful, The Inspirer of Faith 15
7. *Al Muhaymin*, The Guardian of Security 15
8. *Al 'Aziz*, The Almighty, Most Dear 19
9. *Al Jabbar*, The Compeller 22
10. *Al Mutakabbir*, The Supremely Great 22
11. *Al Khaliq*, The Creator 25
12. *Al Bari*, The Evolver, The Patterner 25
13. *Al Musawwir*, The Shaper of Form 25
14. *Al Ghaffar*, The One Who Loves to Forgive 29
15. *Al Qahhar*, The Overwhelming, Irresistible 33
16. *Al Wahhab*, The Ever Giving One, Who Overcomes All Obstacles 37
17. *Ar Razzaq*, The Provider 41
18. *Al Fattah*, The Opener 45
19. *Al 'Alim*, The All Knowing 48
20. *Al Qabid*, The Constrictor 51
21. *Al Basit*, The Expander 51
22. *Al Khafid*, The One Who Brings Low 55
23. *Ar Rafi*, The Exalter 55
24. *Al Mu'izz*, The One Who Bestows Honor 58
25. *Al Mudhill*, The One Who Humbles 58
26. *As Sami*, The All Hearing 62
27. *Al Basir*, The All Seeing 66
28. *Al Hakam*, The Judge 69
29. *Al 'Adl*, The Most Just 73
30. *Al Latif*, The Infinitely Subtle 77

31. *Al Khabir*, The All Aware 80
32. *Al Halim*, The Most Forbearing 83
33. *Al 'Azim*, The Most Magnificent 87
34. *Al Ghafur*, The Oft Forgiving 29
35. *Ash Shakur*, The Grateful, Ever Responsive to Gratitude 91
36. *Al 'Ali*, The Most High 94
37. *Al Kabir*, The Most Great 98
38. *Al Hafiz*, The Preserver 101
39. *Al Muqit*, The Nourisher 107
40. *Al Hasib*, The Reckoner 111
41. *Al Jalil*, The Mightily Majestic 116
42. *Al Karim*, The Infinitely Generous One 119
43. *Ar Raqib*, The Ever Watchful One 123
44. *Al Mujib*, The One Who Responds 126
45. *Al Wasi*, The Infinite, All Encompassing One 130
46. *Al Hakim*, The Most Wise, Healer of All Our Ills 134
47. *Al Wadud*, The Infinitely Loving 137
48. *Al Majeed*, The Sublimely Majestic 141
49. *Al Ba'ith*, The Resurrector 144
50. *Ash Shahid*, The Witness 147
51. *Al Haqq*, The Truth 151
52. *Al Wakil*, The Guardian of All Affairs 154
53. *Al Qawi*, The Source of All Power 157
54. *Al Matin*, The One Who Is Ever Steadfast, Everlastingly Strong 161
55. *Al Wali*, The Friend and Protector 164
56. *Al Hamid*, The One Worthy of All Praise 166
57. *Al Muhsi*, The One Who Keeps Account 172
58. *Al Mubdi*, The Originator Who Creates Out of Nothing 176
59. *Al Mu'id*, The Restorer 180
60. *Al Muhyi*, The One Who Gives Life 184
61. *Al Mumit*, The One Who Takes Life 184
62. *Al Hayy*, The Ever Living 188
63. *Al Qayyum*, The Eternal, Self-Subsisting Source 188
64. *Al Wajid*, The Finder 192
65. *Al Majid*, The Magnificent, Tremendous in Glory 195
66. *Al Wahid*, The One, The Unique 199
67. *Al Ahad*, The One, All Inclusive In Your Unity 199
68. *As Samad*, The Eternal, Satisfier of All Need 203
69. *Al Qadir*, The Pourer of Power 206
70. *Al Muqtadir*, The Determiner 206
71. *Al Muqaddim*, The Expediter 210
72. *Al Mu'akhkhir*, The Delayer 210
73. *Al Awwal*, The First 215

74. *Al Akhir*, The Last 215
75. *Az Zahir*, The Manifest 218
76. *Al Batin*, The Hidden... 218
77. *Al Waali*, The Guardian, Bestower of Bounty.. 223
78. *Al Muta'ali*, The Supremely High.. 223
79. *Al Barr*, The Bestower of Beneficence... 227
80. *At Tawwab*, The One Who Turns Us in Repentance 233
81. *Al Muntaqim*, The Rectifier 236
82. *Al 'Afuw*, The One Who Forgives and Erases the Traces.......................... 29
83. *Ar Rauf*, The Most Kind... 240
84. *Al Malik ul Mulk*, The Sovereign of the Dominion................................... 244
85. *Zhul Jalali wal Ikram*, The Lord of Power and Abundant Beneficence..... 248
86. *Al Muqsit*, The One Who Keeps the Balance, The Equitable.................. 252
87. *Al Jami*, The Gatherer 256
88. *Al Ghani*, The One Who Is Rich, Without Need..................................... 259
89. *Al Mughni*, The Enricher... 259
90. *Al Mani*, The Protector from Harm 227
91. *Ad Darr*, The Creator of the Harmful, The Afflicter 227
92. *An Nafi*, The Creator of All Good 227
93. *An Nur*, The Light.. 263
94. *Al Hadi*, The Guide 268
95. *Al Badi*, The Skilful Original Creator... 272
96. *Al Baqi*, The Truly Abiding One 275
97. *Al Warith*, The Inheritor of All 278
98. *Ar Rashid*, The Most Righteous Teacher 284
99. *As Sabur*, The Most Patient, Inspirer of Patience 288

Index
294

Preface

Bismillah arRahman arRahim

Moments with the Names

"I was a Hidden Treasure, and I so loved to be known
that I created the two worlds, seen and Unseen,
in order that My Treasure of Generosity and Loving-kindness
might be known."
[*Hadith Qudsi*][1]

We offer these reflections on the "Ninety-Nine Names of God,"[2] intrinsic to Islam and the Quranic revelation, to support the increased opening of our awareness to all the Generosity and Loving-kindness of the Divine Bestowal. The Divine is so generous with the qualities of Being that in any moment they may be perceived in new ways, in varied intermingled resonances, with different hues, to touch our hearts and minds and souls and bodies, and awaken us in awe. God willing (*Inshallah*), more windows and doors might open every day for us to witness the Beauty and Magnificence of this Creation, both outwardly and inwardly, bestowed by that One who continually sustains us in every moment, with such an immense outpouring and in-pouring of Love.

We may choose to *zhikr* (repeat/remember, call upon) one of the Names or Qualities of God with our voices and our hearts, and we may, also, use our hands and feet to express them through our actions, recognizing that there is not a thing in this world that is without them. Everything is alive with that Love and manifests it in some aspect. Ninety-Nine Names are

---

1 *Hadith Qudsi*. A communication from the Divine, conveyed through the heart of the Prophet Muhammad, beyond the frame of the Quran.
2 The "Ninety-Nine Names of God" are the collection of "The Most Beautiful Names" or "Qualities" of the Divine that are referenced in the Quran. Within this volume, the transliterated spelling of the Names from the original Arabic has been simplified to enable greater accessibility for diverse readers. The traditional listings of Ninety-Nine Names vary slightly, and it is acknowledged that the Qualities of God are actually far beyond our telling, yet these Ninety-Nine represent a basis for recognition of the unfolding of all the attributes of power and beauty in their interplay throughout creation.

reflected in Name through the Quran, and yet there are infinite hues of the Divine, as, in subtlety, they reflect through all of us.³

Intimations of the Names, as they arrived over recent months within this heart, are included here in twos or threes or more, in clusters or constellations of Names, that we, dear reader, might be encouraged to look and witness again the dancing and singing of all the Names, even beyond the Ninety-Nine here expressed, in all the realms of our existence. For surely, our Beloved Sustainer is ever revealing Himself/Herself/Itself in new ways, in new moments upon the horizons, all around us, and within ourselves.

The Quranic selections included here are excerpted from *The Light of Dawn, Daily Readings from the Holy Qur'an*⁴ or are newly rendered, based upon the work of Yusuf Ali and Muhammad Asad, for whose enlightening labors we are so deeply grateful, in an attempt to elicit again in yet another, fresh way, the Spirit enlivening these messages of Love.

We have used the feminine pronoun and the masculine for both the human being and in reference to God, so that those reading these selections may expand their awareness and be reminded that within the Universe and understanding of the Quran, God is not limited by gender, for *Truly, Our Sustainer is beyond anything by which we may seek to define Him/Her*.⁵ The Quran is one of the few Holy Books with which we are familiar which speaks directly to both *men who have faith* and *women who have faith* in numerous passages. In God's sight, men and women are equal; what matters is not gender, wealth, or power, but that we bring to our Sustainer *a sound heart*⁶ when we return to Our Source. It is these who shall find themselves abiding in the Garden, now and eternally . . . a Garden underneath which rivers flow, and where everywhere one is met with the greeting, *"Peace."*⁷

Sometimes the voice of the Quran comes to us in the first person, *Call upon Me, I will answer.*⁸ Sometimes it comes as a collective "We":

---

3 Within this gathering, we have also included some passages from the Bible, as they sing so much in resonance with the passages from the Quran, and offerings from Mevlana Jalaluddin Rumi (and St. Francis), representative, and in recognition of, the continual unfolding of revelation and inspiration from our Beloved Sustainer, throughout all of humanity, through the unfoldings of generations of life.
4 *The Light of Dawn, Daily Readings from the Holy Qur'an*, Selected and Rendered by Camille Adams Helminski, Shambhala publications, 1998.
5 Quran: 37:180.
6 Quran: 26:89.
7 Quran: 36:58.
8 Quran: 40:60.

We are not asking you to provide sustenance—We provide it for you.[9] Some have understood this "We" as the collective of the attributes or "Names" of God. The Name "Allah" is not included in the traditional list of Ninety-Nine, because it is understood to encompass all the Names within it, as the *Ismi Jalal*, the "Name of Power," used by both Muslims and Christians of Arabic speaking countries to call upon the Divine Reality.

These reflections with the "Names" might be used as the basis for a morning meditation, perhaps to inspire one's own relationship with a Name in that moment unfolding. One might sit quietly after one's morning prayer, and perhaps offer the two morning prayers of the Prophet Muhammad, even as did Mevlana Jalaluddin Rumi in his daily practice, and then read a reflection included here with the accompanying *ayats* (verses, or "signs"), and open one's heart and mind for the inflowing of further inspiration.

We offer this small collection with deep gratitude to our dear friend, Hamida Battla, whose own inspiration assisted in bringing forth this gathering of remembrances, and with gratitude to all the sweet friends whose hearts have called forth these reflections through their love.

As Mevlana Jalaluddin Rumi prayed, we offer this volume:

> In the Name of God the Compassionate, the Merciful,
> whose help we implore and in whom we trust,
> and with whom are the keys to our hearts.[10]
> And God bless Muhammad, and all his family and Companions,
> and all the Messengers of the Beloved!

May that Most Beautiful and Most Gracious One forgive our mistakes and errors and make fruitful this offering that comes to you, dear reader, with so much love from this heart to yours, as together we witness the unfolding of that Greatest Love that supports us every day and night of our lives, embedded in our hearts, awaiting its greatest joy—of seeing each other's beauty and hearing each other's songs of love, in all the manners of their expression, coming to know the resilience of Life, through that Eternal Source.

Subhanallah, Ya Rabb al Alameen! Glory be to God! O Sustainer of All Worlds! Sublimely Amazing is God!

---

9   Quran: 20:131.
10 Mevlana Jalaluddin Rumi, *Mathnawi*, Book V: Prologue.

Ya Nur, Ya Wadud, Ya Karim,
O Light, O Love, O Infinitely Generous One!
Shukrulillah! We give thanks to God, for all the myriad ways of His/Her intimations to us, moment by moment.

~ Camille Hamilton Adams Helminski

1st of Ramadan, 2017

Awakening Prayer of Muhammad
(May peace and blessings be upon him)

We have awakened and all of creation has awakened for God,
Sustainer of all the worlds.
O God, I ask You for the best the day has to offer,
opening, support, light, blessings, guidance,
and I seek refuge in You from any harm in it
and any harm that might come after it.

Prayer of Light
(Du'a'u-Nur)

Prayer of the Prophet Muhammad, recited daily by Mevlana Jalaluddin Rumi[11]

O God! Grant me Light in my heart,
Light in my grave,
Light in front of me, Light behind me,
Light to my right, Light to my left,
Light above me, Light below me,
Light in my ears, Light in my eyes,
Light within my skin, Light in my hair,
Light within my flesh, Light in my blood, Light in my bones.
O God! Increase my Light everywhere.
O God! Grant me Light in my heart, Light on my tongue,
Light in my eyes, Light in my ears,
Light to my right, Light to my left,
Light above me, Light below me,
Light in front of me, Light behind me,
and Light within my self; increase my Light.

---

[11] *The Mevlevi Wird, The Prayers Recited Daily by Mevlevi Dervishes*, Translation of the *Awrad-i Sharif*, offered by Camille Helminski, Threshold Society, 2000. This prayer is very reminiscent of the short version of the beautiful "Breastplate of St. Patrick" prayer from fifth century Ireland.

St. Francis of Assisi's Prayer in Praise of God

*Given to Brother Leo, after Francis's journey to Egypt,
where he was inspired by the expression of the "Ninety-Nine Names"*

You are holy, Lord, the only God,
and Your deeds are wonderful.
You are strong.
You are great.
You are the Most High.
You are Almighty.
You, Holy Father are King of heaven and earth.
You are Three and One, Lord God, all Good.
You are Good, all Good, supreme Good,
Lord God, living and true.
You are love. You are wisdom.
You are humility. You are endurance.
You are rest. You are peace.
You are joy and gladness.
You are justice and moderation.
You are all our riches, and You suffice for us.
You are beauty.
You are gentleness.
You are our protector.
You are our guardian and defender.
You are our courage. You are our haven and our hope.
You are our faith, our great consolation.
You are our eternal life, Great and Wonderful Lord,
God Almighty, Merciful Saviour.

Introduction

Try as you might to put a face on Him (or Her or It), the expansiveness of the whole proposition of a Creator of the Universe exceeds any image you may draw. Yet Islam encourages the pleasures of contemplation. For people who reflect, this possibility of thinking about God is fruitfully facilitated by a spiritual lexicon of modifiers called the "Ninety-Nine Beautiful Names," which, like tangents drawn around a perfect circle, reveal its outline, even while the Circle of the Divine remains unseen.

The Ninety-Nine Beautiful Names of God are attributes of the invisible Bestower. They are the qualities embodied by God, the discernable ways in which He interacts with His Creation. The two best-known of these attributes, the ones invoked at the start of every chapter of the Quran, are The Merciful and The Compassionate. When you experience Mercy, you are experiencing God. When you experience Compassion, you are in the embrace of The Compassionate One.

The Ninety-Nine Beautiful Names are a favorite theme in the art of Arabic calligraphy. They hang on walls in Muslim homes around the world. They are worked into carpets and writ large in tiles on the towering walls of impressive mosques. They are pondered and repeated while praying or walking, driving or flying. They are told on beads the way Catholics tell their rosaries, as a means to draw nearer to the Unknowable, and as a means of self-transformation.

The book before you is a meditation on these attributes, not incised in plaster, fired on tile or told on beads, but inscribed in words on paper, in flows of poetry. Francis of Assisi, it is said, after some months spent among the Muslims of Egypt, was inspired by these Names to translate and concentrate their meanings into a Christian prayer of praise, which he set down in medieval Latin. The following pages arise from their own unique occasion.

These are praise poems—unhesitant, pure, reminiscent in places of the Welsh-English metaphysical poets Henry Vaughan and George Herbert, as when Herbert says, "There is a sweetness in love, ready-penned, write that." Here the poet's faith is the starting point for a surprisingly wide-ranging inspiration, drawing the Ninety-Nine Eternal Qualities into a contemporary context without ever debasing them.

When, for example, "You, the All Hearing" (*As-Sami*) is evoked, the poem begins,

> Ah, the moon is full.
> No wonder I can't sleep

and pulls the poet outdoors into a full moon night of chorusing cicadas. A few lines later the same poem easily makes room for

> This week I learned
> it really matters
> who tunes your piano.

Its roving lines reach into modern life, but they are also ready to draw larger conclusions. From piano strings, the poem moves swiftly to the overtones that linger "of our lives":

> What are we telling ourselves?

Here candor is at the service of a larger project. Soon enough we are being asked to,

> Realign our voices . . .
> into praise,

These poems are inspired by a deep contemplation of Divine attributes, bright as sparks struck off flint, in Camille Hamilton Adams Helminski's blazing encounter with the Ninety-Nine Names of the Beloved.

~ Michael Wolfe,
Author of *One Thousand Roads to Mecca*

The Most Beautiful Names

Bismillah arRahman arRahim

1. Ar Rahman, The Infinitely Compassionate One & 2. Ar Rahim, The Infinitely Merciful One

Ya Rahman, Ya Rahim, Ya Wadud

O You Who Are Infinite Compassion,
Infinite Mercy,
how could we conceive
of the vastness of Your Love?
Every day you nourish us,
every day You support our limbs
as we move through this space
You have given us;
and those whose portion
has become stillness,
still, inwardly, may travel vast distances.
Your Sun shines each day upon us all,
whether in remembrance
or forgetfulness,
Your Compassion holds our hearts
and would inform us
if we would but pause
to receive Your Knowledge—
and the rains come pouring
into these hearts
when we have opened
in thirst these throats
ready to receive Your Mercy,
clear water for those who are longing.
You return us to our origin—
and *everything was created from water*—
Your Mercy comes to know Itself in us,

until *Rahman is seated upon the throne* of the heart,
so that the radiance of that Sunshine
might fill these fragile bones
with strength from the depths
and the heights
of Your Loving,
that like the Prophet Muhammad
we might, also,
become "a mercy to the worlds."
For, *Truly, those who have faith*
and do the deeds of wholeness and healing
the Infinitely Compassionate will endow with love.

Ya Rahman, O Infinitely Compassionate One
(the Sun that shines upon us all),
Ya Rahim, O Infinitely Merciful One
(the Rain of Blessing we receive when we turn and open in receptivity),
Ya Wadud, O Infinitely Loving One

We made out of water every living thing.
[21:30]

O our Sustainer! You embrace all things
within Your Compassion and Knowledge.
Forgive then those who turn in repentance and follow Your Path.
[40:7]

Your Sustainer has willed upon Himself/Herself
the law of Compassion and Mercy.
[6:54]

Say: "Call upon God, or call upon the Infinitely Compassionate:
by whichever name you invoke Him/Her,

His / Hers are all the Most Beautiful Names."[12]
[17:110]

To all who stand in awe, a revelation from Him / Her
who has created the earth and the high heavens,
the Infinitely Compassionate One,
seated on the throne of His / Her almightiness.
[20:3–4]

To God belongs the dominion of the heavens and the earth.
And all things return to God
who merges night into day and merges day into night
and knows completely the secrets of hearts.
[57:5–6]

We have sent you as naught but a mercy for all worlds.
[21:107]

And God sends down water from the skies
and with it bestows life to the earth that was dead:
truly, in this is a sign for those who listen.
[16:65]

My Mercy overwhelms everything.
[7:156]

Truly, those who have faith and do righteous deeds
the Infinitely Compassionate will endow with love.
[Surah Maryam 19:96]

---

12 *Al Asma al-Husna*, "The Most Beautiful Names," all the attributes of perfection, the qualities of the Divine that manifest throughout this creation in all their interplay and assist us in coming to know that Truth of Compassion and Mercy. The root word in Arabic for both The Compassionate (*Rahman*) and The Merciful (*Rahim*), is the triliteral root word for "womb," and all but one of the Surahs (chapters) of the Quran begin with the phrase, *In the Name of God, the Infinitely Compassionate and Merciful (Bismillah arRahman arRahim)*, encouraging us to recognize how we and all the stories of our lives and that of creation are held within the womb of God's nurturing Love.

3. Al Malik, The Sovereign

Ya Malik, Ya Quddus

Each morning we awaken
and watch as You unfurl
all the glories of the day.
Moment by moment
we wait upon Your Word,
O Sovereign, Most Holy One,
who inspire our life, our love,
it is You
who shield us from harm
when we would listen
and turn to You,
within Your Grace.
This Sea of Love is surging,
and we, these little drops,
are swirled together
by the force of Your Loving.
For centuries we have danced,
from generation to generation,
arising now with red hair
and sometimes with brown,
with light skin or skin of darker hue,
but always within, You.
Such mysteries You clarify
when we would look—
how we are all knit together,
strand by strand
of inheritance of genes,
from east and west
and north and south,
that have sailed upon the seas.
When, from time to time,

one tribe has alienated another,
made strangers of themselves,
it has only taken one man
and one woman
from behind the scenes
to fall in love to bring us back
together and interweave
again the pattern of Your Love
to support our sustenance.
Bees fly far and mingle
with flowers of many scents
to bring forth new blooms
and honey that heals.
O Sovereign, Most Holy One,
help us to see
how we are made better
with diversity that purifies
and again renews
all the strands of DNA
that would express You.
"I was a Hidden Treasure,
and I so loved to be known
that I created the two worlds,
seen and Unseen,
in order that My Treasure
of Generosity and Loving-kindness
might be known."
We give thanks for that overflowing
generosity in every shape
and form displayed, all around us,
and the impulses of Loving-kindness
that brighten these hearts.
All glory be to You,
O Most Loving, Ever Living,
Most Holy Sovereign,
Most Pure of Intention and of Being,

Most Compassionate and Merciful,
Allah.

Ya Malik, O Sovereign,
Ya Quddus, O Most Holy One, Pure of Intention and of Being,
Ya Wadud, O Most Loving, *Ya Hayy*, O Ever Living,
Ya Rahman, O Most Compassionate, *Ya Rahim*, O Most Merciful,
Allah, "God," a Name used by both Arabic-speaking Muslims and Christians,
pointing to the Source of All Being encompassing all the Qualities
or "Names" of God

High above all is God, the Sovereign, the Truth!
[20:114]

And the things on this earth
which He/She has multiplied in varying hues:
truly, in this is a sign
for those who celebrate the praises of God.
[16:13]

Limitless in His/Her glory is God who created in pairs
all things that the earth produces
as well as their own humankind
as well as things of which as yet they have no knowledge.
[36:36]

And your Sustainer taught the bee to build its cells
in hills, on trees, and in dwelling places,
then to eat of all that the earth produces
and to skillfully find the spacious paths of its Lord.
There issues from within their bodies a drink of varied hues
containing healing for human beings:
truly, in this is a sign for those who reflect.
[16:68–69]

Many ways of life have passed away before your time.
Go, then, about the earth and see what happened
in the end to those who denied the truth:
here is a clear lesson for all human beings
and a guidance and a counsel for those who are conscious of God.
So do not lose heart, nor fall into despair:
for if you are faithful you are bound to ascend.
[3:137–9]

"I was a Hidden Treasure, and I so loved to be known
that I created the two worlds, seen and Unseen,
in order that My Treasure of Generosity and Loving-kindness
might be known."
[*Hadith Qudsi*][13]

---

13 *Hadith Qudsi*: a Communication of the Divine Reality conveyed through the heart of the Prophet Muhammad, beyond the Quranic revelation.

4. Al Quddus, The Most Holy and Pure

Ya Quddus, Ya Wadud, Ya Hadi, Ya Wakil

Paradise Island
is welcoming us,
beckoning, to come
abide in that Vastness,
beyond the travails
of the mainland,
across the waters of Your blessing—
where one does not grieve,
nor fear,
and gentle talk of Spirit
is all that comes to one's ear.
And He has purchased
of the faithful
their lives and their possessions.
All we are is Yours.
If that is so,
how can we harbor anger?
Or jealousy?
Or pain?
When You would wash us
with Your waters
of Purity,
Ya Quddus—
You who are clear, Holy,
without guile—
melt all our misgivings
and turn these boats of self
into Your clear channel,
beyond the turbulence,
guiding us straight
into the Port

of Your Love.
Ya Wadud,
Ya Quddus,
Ya Hadi,
Ya Haqq, Ya Wakil.

Ya Quddus, O Most Pure and Holy,
Ya Wadud, O Infinitely Loving One,
Ya Hadi, O Guide, *Ya Haqq*, O Truth,
Ya Wakil, O Guardian of All Our Affairs

See how God has purchased of the faithful their lives and their possessions;
in return, theirs is the Garden, and so they struggle in God's way.
[9:111]

To those who receive guidance, He/She increases their guidance
and causes them to grow in God-consciousness.
[47:17]

Those who repent, and have faith, and work righteousness:
these will enter the Garden, and will not be wronged in any way—
Everlasting Gardens, those which the Infinitely Compassionate has promised
to His/Her servants in the Unseen:
for His/Her promise must be fulfilled.
They will not hear any empty talk there but only greetings of peace;
and there they will receive their sustenance, morning and evening.
Such is the Garden which We bestow as an inheritance
to those of Our Servants who are conscious of Us.
[19:60–63]

Those will prosper who purify themselves
and remember the Name of their Sustainer and pray.
[87:14–15]

*Truly: all who surrender their whole being to God,
and do good, shall have their reward with their Sustainer;
these need have no fear, neither shall they grieve.*
[2:112]

*Whatever is in the heavens and the earth
declares the praises and glory of God,
the Sovereign, the Most Holy, the Almighty, the Truly Wise.*
[62:1]

5. As Salaam, The One Who Is Peace

Ya Salaam, Ya Mumin, Ya Muhaymin

O You Who Are Eternal
and Ever Present Peace,
renew us with Your breath breathing us,
that restores, that harmonizes
all the parts of our being,
that we might see afresh,
Ya Mumin, Ya Muhaymin,
O You Who Are the Inspirer
and Preserver of Faith,
the True Means of Our Security.
Continually, You invite us
into the abode of Peace,
through the doorway
of Your Awareness
with such care of every aspect
of our being and that of every creature
on the earth, in the sky and the seas,
and, far beyond our sight,
inward and outward,
all that which is hidden.
Ya Salaam, with Your Peace
You protect us,
and in collaboration
we find new words to express
our love for each other and for You
who are the Source of our existence.
Alphabets emerge
of movement and of voice.
With new characters of expression,
we rejoice to find expanded meaning
dancing through the realms.

May we not limit ourselves
with blindered vision,
for You are everywhere.
Ya Khabir,
peace comes through recognition,
when each soul is seen,
Ya Basir.
It is then we are secure
in faith, in trust
in Your bestowal
through each and every thing
birthed into being,
even stones
which are so ancient, anchoring
our earth
and speaking
to those who have hearts to hear.[14]

Ya Salaam, O You Who Are Eternal and Ever Present Peace,
Ya Mumin, O You Who Are the Inspirer and Preserver of Faith,
Ya Muhaymin, O You Who Are the True Means of Our Security,
Ya Samad, O Eternal Self-Subsisting Source of Our Existence,
Satisfier of Our Need,
Ya Khabir, O You Who Are All Aware,
Ya Basir, O You Who Are All Seeing,
Ya Sami, O You Who Are All Hearing

O you who have faith!
celebrate God's praises, and do this often;
and glorify Him morning and evening.
He it is who sends blessings on you as do His angels

---

[14] It is said that the Prophet Muhammad, peace and blessings be upon him, even before the opening of his prophethood, would hear stones speaking. Even so, in many native cultures, around the earth, the wise comprehend.

that He may bring you out of the depths of Darkness into the Light:
and He is Full of Mercy to the faithful.
Their greeting on the Day they meet Him will be "Peace!"
And He has readied for them a most generous recompense.
[33:41–44]

For, servants of the Most Compassionate
are they who walk gently on earth,
and who, whenever the foolish address them, reply with peace;
and who remember their Sustainer far into the night,
prostrating themselves and standing.
[25: 63–64]

O My servants who have faith!
Truly, My earth is spacious, so serve Me alone.
Every soul shall have a taste of death:
in the end to Us shall you all be brought back.
But those who have faith and do good deeds,
to them shall We give a home in the Garden—
lofty mansions beneath which rivers flow—to dwell there always,
an excellent reward for those who act rightly—
those who persevere in patience
and put their trust in their Sustainer.
[29:56–59]

Limitless is He/She in His/Her glory,
and sublimely, immeasurably exalted
above anything people may say.
The seven heavens acclaim His/Her limitless glory,
and the earth, and all that they contain;
and there is nothing that does not celebrate
His/Her immeasurable glory—
but you fail to grasp the manner of their glorifying Him/Her!
[17:43–44]

Bless the Lord, O my soul:
and all that is within me, bless His Holy Name.
Bless the Lord, O my soul, and forget not all His benefits:
who forgives all your errors;
who heals all your disease;
who redeems your life from destruction;
who crowns you with loving-kindness and tender mercies.
[The Bible, Psalm 103:1–4]

God invites to the Abode of Peace;
He/She guides those that will to a way that is straight.
To those who do good is a good recompense, even more!
No darkness nor shame shall veil their faces!
They are companions of the Garden; there will they dwell!
[10:25–26]

6. Al Mumin, The Most Faithful, The Inspirer of Faith & 7. Al Muhaymin, The Guardian of Security

Ya Mumin, Ya Muhaymin, Ya Wadud, Ya 'Alim

Ya Mumin
O You Who Are Most Faithful,
Who Inspire Faith within our hearts,
within our souls!
We know
where
we are tethered,
and trust
deeply
within You.
We hear You
resounding
with every beat of our hearts,
that You have crafted with Your Wisdom,
two chambers in,
two chambers out,
matching love for Love
and bringing sustenance,
to every particle of being
that vibrates with the angels,
"Yes!"
We hear and we bow
in obedience,
in following the Path of Your Love
as every palm tree
knows,
as it lifts Your fronds,
into the fruitfulness of Your Breeze—
we are returning to You
who gave us being.

Let us gift it back again,
with joy
and thanksgiving
for the every-day blessing
of seeing Your Face,
here among us
and upon the horizon,
every time
we look
with Your Eyes,
O Most Gracious
of the Merciful,
we grasp Your Hand
and give thanks.

Ya Mumin, O You Who Are Most Faithful, O Inspirer of Faith,
Ya Muhaymin, O Guardian of Security,
Ya Wadud, O Infinitely Loving One,
Ya 'Alim, O All Knowing One

The Messenger, and the faithful with him,
have faith in what has been revealed to him by his Sustainer:
they all have faith in God, and His/Her angels,
and His/Her revelations, and His/Her messengers,
making no distinction between any of His/Her messengers;
and they say: "We have heard, and we pay heed.
Grant us Your forgiveness, O our Sustainer,
for with You is all journeys' end!"
[2:285]

The faithful are those
whose hearts tremble with awe whenever God is mentioned,
and whose faith is strengthened
whenever His/Her signs are conveyed to them,

and who place their trust in their Sustainer—
those who are constant in prayer
and spend on others out of what We provide for them as sustenance:
In truth, these are the faithful!
They shall have stations of dignity with their Sustainer,
and forgiveness, and a most generous provision.
[8:2–4]

For men and women who surrender themselves to God,
for men and women of faith,
for devout men and women, for true men and women,
for men and women who are patient and persevering,
for men and women who humble themselves before God,
for men and women who give in charity,
for men and women who fast,
for men and women who guard their chastity,
and for men and women who remember God unceasingly,
for them has God readied forgiveness and a supreme recompense.
[33:35]

A Sign for them is the earth that is dead—
We bring it to life and bring forth grain from it of which you may eat.
And We produce there gardens with date-palms and vines
and We cause springs to gush forth from within it,
that they may enjoy the fruits thereof.
It was not their hands that made this;
will they not then give thanks?
[36:33–35]

To God belong the east and the west.
Wherever you turn, there is the Face of God.
Witness, God is Infinite, All Knowing.
[2:115]

Let there be no compulsion in matters of faith.
Right wayfaring stands clearly apart from error:

and so, whoever turns away from the powers of evil and has faith in God
has indeed grasped the most trustworthy handhold
which shall never give way:
for God is All Hearing, All Knowing.
[2:256]

8. Al ʿAziz, The Almighty, Most Dear

Ya ʿAziz, Ya Hakim

O You Who Are Most Dear
and hold us dear within Your Heart,
close beside You,
never will You let us part,
for You are Almighty.
Perhaps we may wander,
unaware of how precious
Your waiting companionship
might be—
sometimes
bright objects mislead us,
when we mistake the glitter
for the gold,
for You have given us freedom,
yet always we are returned
into Your Presence,
for You care
for all that is,
Ever Giving through all obstacles,
guiding us Home.
Ya ʿAziz, Ya Hakim,
You Who Are Almighty and Forever Wise,
depicting stories in ways we can only surmise,
for You are the Artist
beyond
all expertise,
and our knowledge
can only barely glimpse
the range and subtlety
of Your Talent,
O Skilful Creator, Ya Badi.

Hold us close, O Dear One.
Help us to forget our forgetfulness
and remember
that we are born
for intimacy[15]
with You,
who are our Most Beloved
Beloved.
Ya 'Aziz,
Ya Hakim,
Ya Wahhab,
Ya Hadi,
Ya Badi,
Ya Wadud.

Ya 'Aziz, O Almighty One, Most Dear,
Ya Hakim, O Most Wise, Healer of All Our Ills,
Ya Wahhab, O Ever Giving One, Who Overcomes All Obstacles,
Ya Hadi, O Guide, *Ya Badi*, O Skilful Creator,
Ya Wadud, O Infinitely Loving One

Truly, nothing on earth or in the heavens is hidden from God.
He / She it is who shapes you in the wombs as He / She wills.
There is no deity except Him / Her,
the Almighty, the Truly Wise.
[3:5–6]

Strive hard in God's cause with your possessions and your lives:
this is for your own good—if you but knew it!
He / She will forgive you your mistakes,
and will admit you into gardens through which running waters flow,
and into goodly mansions in gardens of perpetual bliss:

---

15 The word for "human being" in Arabic, *insan*, holds within it both the meaning of "one who is forgetful" and "one who has the capacity for intimacy."

that will be the triumph supreme!
And He / She will grant you yet another thing that you dearly love:
support from God, and an opening soon to come;
and so give a glad tiding to all who have faith.
O you who have attained to faith! Be helpers—
even as Jesus, the son of Mary, said unto the white-garbed ones,
"Who will be my helpers in God's cause?"—
whereupon the white-garbed ones replied,
"We shall be helpers of God!"
[61:11–14]

He / She comprehended in His / Her design
the sky which had been as smoke.
He / She said to it and to the earth:
"Come together willingly or unwillingly."
They said: "We come in willing obedience."
So He / She completed them as seven heavens in two aeons
and He / She assigned to each heaven its duty and command.
And We adorned the lower heaven with lights
and provided it with protection.
Such is the Command of the Almighty, the All Knowing.
[41:11–12]

God has caused faith to be dear to you,
and has given it beauty within your hearts,
and has made unbearable to you all denial of the Truth,
and all ill-doing, and all rising against the good.
Such indeed are they who follow the right course
through God's bounty and favor;
and God is All Knowing, Truly Wise.
[49:7–8]

The foremost shall be the foremost —
they who were drawn close unto God!
In gardens of bliss.
[56:10–12]

9. Al Jabbar, The Compeller
& 10. Al Mutakabbir, The Supremely Great

Ya Jabbar, Ya Mutakabbir, Ya Wadud, Ya Hakim

O You Who Compel Us
towards ultimate greatness,
You Who Are Supreme
in knowing and in love,
You knit us together
by bone
and by vibration,
restoring hearts
and limbs
that have been wounded.
Sometimes we trip,
and fall
in our wanderings—
bring us home
to Your Love.
Intertwine us with Your Will
in the best resonance
that rearranges all our cells
and our relations.
The sound of Your Voice
through us heals us;
the water of our being
is stirred to realign
with Your Word,
You Who Are the Knowing Healer,
Ya Hakim.

Ya Jabbar, O Compelling One, You Who Knit Bones Back Together,
Ya Mutakabbir, O You Who Are Supreme,
Ya Wadud, O Infinitely Loving One,
Ya Hakim, O All Wise, Knowing Healer

*God is He/She other than whom there is no god,
who knows what is hidden and what is manifest;
Hu[16], the Infinitely Compassionate, the Infinitely Merciful.
God is He/She other than whom there is no god,
the Sovereign, the Holy One, the Source of Peace,
the Inspirer of Faith, the Preserver of Security,
the Exalted in Might, the Compelling, the Supreme:
Glory to God, who is subtly amazing,
beyond the partners they attribute to Him/Her—
He/She is God, the Creator, the Evolver, the Bestower of Forms.
To Hu belong the Most Beautiful Names:
whatever is in the heavens and on earth declares His/Her Praises and Glory,
and He/She is the Exalted in Might, the All Wise.*
[59:22–24]

*Say: "As for me, I have been commanded
to serve the Sustainer of this City,[17]
the One who has sanctified it
and to whom all things belong.*
[27:91]

*He/She is God: there is no god but He/She—
to Him/Her belongs all praise at the first and at the last:*

---

16 *Hu*: the pronoun of Divine Presence. All words in Arabic have a gender grammatically ascribed to them as they do in French and Spanish, etc. Although Allah is referred to with the third person masculine pronoun *Hu* (*Huwa*), it is universally understood that Allah's Essence is beyond gender or indeed any qualification. In this translation occasionally *Hu* will be used and sometimes "He/She" in an attempt to avoid the mistake of attributing human gender to That which is beyond all our attempts at definition, limitless in subtle glory.

17 I.e. Mecca, where the first temple devoted to the One God was built originally by Abraham. "City" here also has the resonant meaning of "the whole human being"—body, mind, and heart.

His / Hers is the Command, and to Him / Her shall you all return.
[28:70]

*God grants firmness to those who have come to faith
through the word that is unshakably true,
in this world as well as in the life to come.*
[14:27]

11. Al Khaliq, The Creator
& 12. Al Bari, The Evolver and Patterner
& 13. Al Musawwir, The Shaper of Form

Ya Khaliq, Al Bari, Al Mussawir, Ya Wakil, Ya Wadud

O Creator,
You through whom pattern emerges,
who give us shape
and make our shapes beautiful,
we ask You
to be the Guardian of Our Affairs,
to find the Most Beautiful Solutions.
Why does our vision
become so constricted,
when Your Creativity is dancing
all around us
and within
the very atoms of our being?
Ya Bari,
the patterns You unfold
take on new meanings
every moment.
To You belong
the Most Beautiful Names,
O Allah,
and everything You display before us
arises from an Inner Truth.
You who are witness
to all things,
remind us
that Your Creativity circulates
through our arteries and veins;
that Your Creativity

is endless—
and that there are ways
through
tight passages
with Your assistance;
for You are the Beginning
and the End,
the Best Inheritor of all—
everything returns to You,
to be remade,
reformed, refreshed
in Your Beauty,
O Love.
You reunite
the disparate,
Ya Jami;
when we fall away
from our center,
You bring us back
together.
Al Awwal,
Al Akhir,
Al Warith,
O You Who Are Beauty
and Love the beautiful.
Ya Shahid,
Ya Jamil,
Ya Wadud.

Ya Khaliq, O Creator, *Al Bari*, Evolver, Designer of Pattern, *Al Musawwir*, Bestower of Form, *Ya Wakil*, O Guardian of All, *Ya Wadud*, O Infinitely Loving One, *Ya Jami*, O Gatherer, *Al Awwal*, The First, *Al Akhir*, The Last, *Al Warith*, The Inheritor of All, *Ya Jamil*, O You Who Are Beauty, *Ya Shahid*, O Witness

He/She is God, the Creator, the Evolver,
who Shapes all forms and appearances!
His/Hers are the Most Beautiful Names.
All that is in the heavens and on earth extols His/Her limitless glory:
for He/She alone is Almighty, Truly Wise!
[59:24]

It is God who has made the earth a resting-place for you
and the sky a canopy, and has shaped you—
and made your shapes beautiful—
and provided for you sustenance out of the good things of life.
Such is God, your Sustainer:
how full of blessing is God, the Sustainer of all the worlds!
[40:64]

Such is God, your Sustainer:
there is no deity save Him/Her, the Creator of everything.
Then worship Him/Her alone—
for it is He/She who is the Guardian of everything.
[6:102]

And He/She it is who has created the heavens and the earth
in accordance with an inner Truth.
[6:73]

O children of Adam! Beautify yourselves for every act of worship,
and eat and drink, but do not waste:
truly, He/She does not love the wasteful!
Say: "Who can forbid the beauty
which God has brought forth for His/Her servants,
and the pure things from among the means of sustenance?"
Say: "They are in the life of this world for all
those who have attained to faith—
to be theirs alone on the Day of Standing Straight."
[7:31–32]

He/She is the First and the Last,
and the Outward as well as the Inward:
and He/She has full knowledge of everything.
He/She it is who has created the heavens and the earth in six aeons,
and is established on the throne of His/Her almightiness.
He/She knows all that enters the earth, and all that comes out of it,
as well as all that descends from the skies, and all that ascends to them.
And He/She is with you wherever you may be;
and God sees all that you do.
His/Hers is the dominion over the heavens and the earth;
and everything is returning to God.
[57:3–5]

"God is Beauty and loves the beautiful."
[*Hadith* of the Prophet Muhammad]

14. Al Ghaffar, The One Who Loves to Forgive
& 34. Al Ghafur, The Oft Forgiving
& 82. Al 'Afuw, The One Who Forgives and Erases the Traces of Our Error

Ya Ghaffar, Ya Ghafur, Ya 'Afuw

As though it had never been….
What does it take
to clear the past
of pain?
A heart full of longing
for Peace,
and Your imagining
of a time
that did not transpire,
that breathes
afresh,
empty of histories
of our tangled weavings,
where new possibilities
await.
We, through You,
can imagine
another story,
one that does not hurt
to remember;
how do we do that,
for ourselves,
our parents,
our children?
Erase the footprints
in the sands of our hearts,
and let the water

of Your Grace
bubbling up
wash the chambers
of reflection
that keep track
of memories.
Remember the kindness—
and when resistance arises—
thinking again,
we might be fooled—
remember: You
are our only Protector,
Ya Wali, Ya Wakil,
Ya 'Afuw.
We must rely on You,
for our human
will is too fickle,
no matter
how much
we may try
to be True—
You alone do we ask for help—
guard our hearts,
do not let us stray.
Purify our intentions,
keep us close to You,
O Beloved,
O Rectifying,
Oft Forgiving,
Love,
we will know we are truly forgiven
when no inkling
remains on the paper
of the novel of our lives,
and it is only Your Nobility
that shines,

now
and when the sun sets.
May the underlying Truth
of our story be preserved,
with You,
Ya 'Afuw.

Ya Ghaffar, O You Who Love to Forgive,
Ya Ghafur, O Oft Forgiving One,
Ya 'Afuw, O You Who Absolve and Erase All Our Error,
Ya Wali, O Friend and Protector,
Ya Wakil, O Guardian of All Our Affairs,
Ya Haqq, O Truth

*Strive among yourselves to attain your Sustainer's forgiveness
and a paradise as vast as the heavens and the earth,
which has been readied for those who are conscious of God—
who spend in His way in times of abundance and in times of hardship,
and hold in check their anger,
and pardon their fellow human beings,
because God loves those who do good;
and who, when they have committed a shameful deed
or have otherwise wronged their own souls,
remember God
and pray for forgiveness for their mistakes—
for who can forgive sins but God?—
and do not knowingly persist
in doing whatever wrong they may have done.*
[3:133–5]

*"Ask your Sustainer to forgive you your sins,
and then turn towards Him/Her in repentance—
for, truly, my Sustainer is Infinitely Merciful, a Fount of Love!"*
[11:90, words of the Prophet Shu'ayb]

*"Seek the forgiveness of your Sustainer,
for He / She is the One Who Loves to Forgive."*
[71:10, words of the Prophet Noah]

You alone do we ask for help.
[1:5]

*"O Moses! Fear not—for, behold,
no fear need the message-bearers have in My Presence,
and neither need anyone who has done wrong
and then has replaced the wrong with good:
for, truly, I am Much Forgiving, Infinitely Merciful!*
[27:10–11]

*O you who have attained to faith!
Remain conscious of God and have faith in His / Her messenger,
and He / She will grant you a double portion of His / Her Mercy:
He / She will provide for you a light by which you shall walk,
and He / She will forgive you:
For God is Ever Ready to Forgive and is the Most Merciful.*
[57:28]

*Behold, God is indeed an Eraser of Sins, Oft Forgiving.
Thus it is, because God makes the night grow longer by shortening the day,
and makes the day grow longer by shortening the night;
and because God is All Hearing, All Seeing.
Thus it is, because God alone is the Ultimate Truth.*
[22:60–62]

15. Al Qahhar, The Overwhelming Irresistible One

Al Qahhar, Al Wahid, Al Wadud

You are the Creator
of all things,
the One,
the Supreme,
who overcomes
all our inhibitions
and our obstacles,
all that blocks our way,
inwardly
or outwardly,
resolving
all our issues,
and issuing grace
through the fissures
in these mountains
that hold firm
through Your Power
even under the force
of Your explosive
Love—
new life
comes
as a surprise
from Your Smile,
the warmth
of Your Sun
shining,
even as Your rain
falls
and frothy with the air
of Your Breath

pours
down the mountainside.
For those who respond
to their Lord
are all good things.
How could we resist
Your irresistible
attraction,
Your Overwhelming
Grace,
the joy
of seeing Your Face
reflected
on these mountains,
shining from the forests
wet
with the dew
of Your kiss?
Glory be to You,
the One, the Irresistible,
You who gather
and compress us
into recognition
of Your Oneness
that ties us all together
through Your Breath,
through Your Ever-Enlivening Love,
and we are born
before Your Glance,
in all Your Purity,
standing
now
in Truth,
Ya Quddus al Haqq,
Ya Wahid al Qahhar,
Ya Wadud.

Al Qahhar, The Overwhelming Irresistible One,
Ya Quddus, O Most Holy and Pure, *Al Haqq,* The Truth,
Ya Wahid, O One, Unique,
Ya Wadud, O Infinitely Loving One

Glory be to You, the One, the Overwhelming, Irresistible!
He/She it is who has created the heavens and the earth
in accordance with [an inner] Truth.
He/She causes the night to flow into the day,
and causes the day to flow into the night;
and He/She has made the sun and the moon in service,
each running its course for a determined term.
Is not He/She the Almighty, the All Forgiving?
[39:4–5]

Say: "God is the Creator of all things;
and He/She is the One who holds absolute sway over all that exists."
He/She sends down water from the sky,
and river-beds run high according to their measure . . .
In this way does God set forth the parables of those who have responded
to their Sustainer with a goodly response.
[13:16–18]

He/She rewards those who do good with what is most beautiful.
[53:31]

For He/She is the Irresistible, above His/Her servants,
and He/She is the Truly Wise Healer, All Aware.
[6:18]

It was Our power that caused the mountains and the birds
to join David in celebrating Our limitless glory.
[21:79]

*Whoever has faith and does the deeds of wholeness and reconciliation—
he or she shall have a goodly reward, and easy will be his or her task
as We order it by our Command.*
[18:88]

*"O soul in complete rest and satisfaction!
Return to your Sustainer, well-pleased and well-pleasing!
Enter then among My devoted ones—yes, enter My Garden!"*
[89:27–30]

16. Al Wahhab, The Ever Giving One, Who Overcomes All Obstacles

Ya Wahhab, Al Qahhar, Ya Wadud, Al Fattah, Al Muqit, Al Wasi, Ya Rahim

You overcome us,
to give us all that is nourishing,
opening our mouths
to receive Your Love
in all its flavors and tastes—
Ya Wadud,
He/She loves them,
and they love Him/Her;
Your Love comes first.
It has given us being.
You have given us hearts
with which to perceive You,
and all the subtleties of nature
and our fellow men and women.
How could these eyes
even know what they are seeing
without these hearts beating,
registering within the brain,
and recognizing, "Yes,
you are a tree"—
It is *You who splits open the kernels*
and causes the plants to sprout forth;
glories, glories abound
every morning
as the light returns.
Ya Wahhab,
O You Who Give without stinting,
keep turning us
around You,

and open the eye of these hearts
to witness the continuous
outpouring and inpouring
of Your Overwhelming
and Infinitely Nourishing
Love,
that flows every morning,
and evening, every moment,
held with Your Mercy
encompassing us all.

Al Wahhab, The Ever Giving One, Who Overcomes All Obstacles,
Al Qahhar, The One Who Overwhelms us with Grace,
Ya Wadud, O Infinitely Loving One,
Al Fattah, The Opener, *Al Muqit*, The Nourisher,
Al Wasi, The All Encompassing One, *Ya Rahim*, O Infinitely Merciful One

*He / She loves them,
and they love Him / Her.*
[5:54]

*And God has given you mates of your own kind
and has given you, through your mates,
children and children's children,
and has provided for you sustenance out of the good things of life.*
[16:72]

*Truly, it is God who splits open the kernels
and allows the seeds to sprout forth,
bringing forth the living out of the dead.*
[6:95]

*It is He / She who has created for you
hearing, sight, feeling, and understanding.*
[23:78]

*"Establish for us what is good, in this world as well as hereafter—
see how we have turned towards You!"*
*God's word came: "With my Stringency I try whom I will,
but even so, My Mercy encompasses everything.
And so I shall confer it upon those who are regardful of Me,
and share of their abundance, and have faith in our signs."*
[7:156]

*Don't you see that God has made in service to you
all that is in the heavens and on earth
and has made His/Her bounties flow to you
in abundant measure, seen and unseen?*
[31:20]

*And in all the many hues which He/She has created for you on earth—
in this, behold, there is a sign for people who take it to heart!
And He/She it is who has made the sea in service,
so that you might eat fresh meat from it,
and take from it adornments which you may wear,
and you see ships making a way through it,
so that you might love to seek His/Her bounty,
and thus have cause to be grateful.*
[16:13–14]

*So glorify God when you reach the evening
and when you rise in the morning;
for all praise belongs to Him/Her in the heavens and on earth,
and also in the late afternoon and when the day passes its zenith.
It is He/She who brings out the living from the dead
and who brings out the dead from the living,
and who gives life to the earth after it has died,
and even so shall you all be brought forth.*
[30:17–19]

*He/She it is who has bestowed upon you from on high this Book,
containing clear messages . . .*

"O our Sustainer!
Do not let our hearts swerve from the Truth after You have guided us;
and bestow on us the gift of Your Grace:
truly, You are the Continual Giver of Gifts."
[3:7–8]

17. Ar Razzaq, The Provider of All

Ya Razzaq, Ya Muqit, Ya Salaam, Ya Wadud

O Provider of All,
You nourish us
with peace,
with healing—
*You give us to eat and to drink;
it is You who heal us
when we are ill—*
mustering all the forces
of the angels to our aid,
uplifting our hearts
with the songs of Your Love.
Ya Wadud, Ya Razzaq,
let us, also, feed the hungry,
giving of the best
we have to give,
not neglecting the stranger
or our next of kin,
extending our hearts
in welcome
to Your Abundance
that is seeking us
even more than
we are seeking it,
for You would have us know
the elegant and incredible Beauty
of Your Vast and Deepest Being
incredible only
because these limited eyes
can only see
so far, until
Your Grace

transforms
our vision
through Your Sight,
Ya Basir.
We give thanks,
Hallelujah,
Alhamdulillah—
in every tongue
that speaks and drinks
of Your Wisdom.
You will understand
even without words
for You know our hearts
from the moment
they first began to beat
in these chests
of Your Love,
O You who hold the keys
to storehouses
of all these vessels
of Your Love
and pour it without measure,
yet apportioning to need,
and providing beyond all reckoning
through these hearts
that have been made
to know You,
to open in awe,
to serve and to heal,
breathing in the Peace
of that Vastness
and breathing out Your Love.
Ya Salaam, Ya Wasi,
Ya Wadud, Ya Karim,
Ya Razzaq, Ya Muqit,
Ya Muqsit, Ya Mu'id,

Ya Basir, Ya Sami,
Ya 'Alim, Ya Hakim,
Ya Shafi.

Ya Razzaq, O Provider of All, *Ya Muqit*, O Nourisher,
Ya Salaam, O You Who Are Peace, *Ya Wadud*, O Infinitely Loving One,
Ya Wasi, O All Encompassing and All Pervading One,
Ya Karim, O Infinitely Generous One,
Ya Muqsit, O Equitable One, *Ya Mu'id*, O You Who Restore,
Ya Basir, O All Seeing One, *Ya Sami*, O All Hearing One,
Ya 'Alim, O All Knowing One,
Ya Hakim, O Wisest of the Wise, You Who Heal All Our Ills,
Ya Shafi, O You Who Grant Healing, and Cure Us[18]

God is He/She other than whom there is no god,
who knows what is hidden and what is manifest;
Hu, the Infinitely Compassionate, the Infinitely Merciful.
God is He/She other than whom there is no god,
the Sovereign, the Holy One, the Source of Peace.
[59:22]

And We have spread the earth out wide;
set upon it firm and immovable mountains;
and produced upon it all kinds of things in balance.
And We have provided there means of subsistence for you
and for those whose provision does not depend on you.
And there is not a thing but its storehouses are with Us,
but We only send it down in appropriate measure.
[15:19–21]

---

18 *Ya Shafi, Ya Kafi, Ya Muafi*—"O Healer, You Who Cure Us, O You Who Are Enough, O Healer and Restorer" is a prayer offered for healing, including Names beyond the traditional list of the Ninety-Nine Names, acknowledging the total healing capacity of the Divine to restore us better than before any illness. It is derived from the prayers of the Prophet Muhammad, and the Quranic verse: *Is not God enough for His/Her servants?* [39:36]

And I have not created the invisible beings and human beings
except that they may adore Me—
no sustenance do I ask of them, nor do I demand that they feed Me.
For, truly, God Himself/Herself is the Provider of All Sustenance,
the Source of All Power, the Eternally Steadfast!
[51:56–58]

"The Sustainer of all the worlds,
who has created me and is the One who guides me,
and is the One who gives me to eat and to drink,
and, when I fall ill, is the One who restores me to health."
[26:77–80, words of the Prophet Abraham]

"When my faithful servant draws near to me
with voluntary acts of devotion,
then I love him or her,
and I become the ears with which he or she hears,
the eyes with which he or she sees,
the hand with which he or she touches,
the foot with which he or she walks."
[*Hadith Qudsi*]

Never shall you attain righteousness unless you spend on others
out of what you yourselves truly love;
and whatever you spend—certainly, God knows.
[3:92]

See how God grants sustenance to whom He/She wills, beyond all reckoning.
[3:37, words of Blessed Mary, Mother of Jesus]

Those who have faith and do the deeds of wholeness and reconciliation
will be brought into gardens beneath which running waters flow,
there to dwell by their Sustainer's consent,
and will be welcomed with the greeting, "Peace!"
[14:23]

18. Al Fattah, The Opener

Ya Fattah, Ya 'Alim, Ya Wadud

O Opener of Gifts,
You who open the way
when we are lost,
who provide the key
when we have forgotten
the treasure,
and open wide vistas
of new worlds
from the tightness
of our enclosure,
so many times
You have cleared our path—
how could we forget
all the beauties
of Your Graciousness?
And the strength
with which You move us,
surging
through the dams of our conceptions,
to the Ocean of Your Love!
Ah, water moves downward
wherever there is thirst,
and, yet, it also moves upward
into Your Heavens.
You keep opening
our hearts
that we might know You
in all directions.
Ya 'Alim, You Who Know
and understand all tongues,
Your language

perceives us,
and we find ourselves
in Your Arms
that open so wide,
every moment,
to receive us,
Subhanallah!
Ya Fattah,
Ya 'Alim,
Ya Wadud.

Ya Fattah, O Opener,
Ya 'Alim, O All Knowing One,
Ya Wadud, O Infinitely Loving One,
Subhanallah! Glory be to God!

God is the Creator of all things,
and He/She alone has the power to determine the fate of all things.
His/Hers are the keys to the mysteries of the heavens and the earth.
[39:62–63]

And He/She it is who makes the night as a robe for you,
and sleep as repose, and makes every day a resurrection.
And He/She it is who sends the winds as heralds of glad tidings
preceding His/Her Mercy.
And We send down purifying water from the sky
that with it We may give life to a dead land
and assuage the thirst of things We have created.
[25:47-49]

And among His/Her wonders is this:
He/She creates for you mates out of your own kind,
so that you might incline towards them,
and He/She engenders love and tenderness between you:

in this, behold, there are messages indeed for people who reflect!
And among His/Her wonders is the creation of the heavens and the earth,
and the diversity of your tongues and colors:
for in this, behold, there are messages indeed
for all who are possessed of knowing!
[30:21–22]

Consider the heavens, ever-revolving,
and the earth, bursting open with plants and water!
Behold, this is indeed a word that distinguishes truth and falsehood,
and is not a fruitless tale.
[86:11–14]

Say: "Our Sustainer will bring us all together,
and then He/She will lay open the truth between us, in justice—
for He/She alone is the One Who Opens all Truth, the All Knowing!"
[34:26]

19. Al 'Alim, The All Knowing

Ya 'Alim, Ya Fattah, Ya Rahman, Ya Rauf, Ya Wadud

Ya Rahman,
so unlimited is Your Compassion
that every day You show us
ways we may fall short
and help us
to see
how to open
our hearts.
Ya Fattah,
You Who Open
the gateways of the Unseen,
with Your Knowledge
You comprehend
the best moment
for each unfolding, Ya 'Alim.
It is You who release
the child from the womb,
You who open the door
into this world
and the way of our return.
You know what is in our hearts,
whether we speak
or we are silent.
The trees, with all their leaves,
have stories to tell
of all You have told them,
and deep within their roots
Your Knowledge
guides them
to find nourishment
through this earth,

that lends us all support.
O dear sweet Lord,
there is so much
for which to offer thanks!
How can we possibly encompass
all You would give,
unless we relinquish
this construct of "self,"
and, washed with the waters
of Your Knowing,
become completely Yours,
with open-heart,
poured out again
with, and by, Your Love.

Ya 'Alim, O All Knowing One, *Ya Fattah*, O You Who Open,
Ya Rahman, O Infinitely Compassionate One,
Ya Rauf, O Infinitely Tender and Kind,
Ya Wadud, O Infinitely Loving One

*Hu knows all that is before them and all that is hidden from them,
but they cannot encompass Him/Her with their knowledge.
All faces shall be humbled
before the Ever Living, the Self-Subsisting, the Eternal:
hopeless indeed will be the one who carries corruption,
but the one who acts rightly and has faith
need have no fear of harm
nor of any lessening of what is due him/her.
And so we have sent down this, an Arabic Quran,
and explained in it in detail some guidelines
so that they may stand in awe of God
or that it may cause remembrance in them.
High above all is God, the Sovereign, the Truth!
Do not be hasty with the Quran*

before its revelation to you is complete,
but say: "O my Sustainer! Increase me in knowing."
[20:110–114]

Truly, God knows all the hidden things
of the heavens and the earth—
truly, He/She has complete knowledge of all that is within hearts.
[35:38]

If one does more good than he/she is bound to do,
see how God is Responsive to Gratitude, All Knowing.
[2:158]

Are you not aware that it is God whose limitless glory
all creatures in the heavens and on earth praise,
even the birds as they outspread their wings?
Indeed, each of them knows
how to pray to Him/Her and glorify Him/Her;
and God has Full Knowledge of all that they do:
for God's is the Sovereignty of the heavens and the earth,
and with God is all journeys' end.
[24:41–42]

God is Infinitely Tender and Kind with His/Her servants.
[2:207]

20. Al Qabid, The Constrictor
& 21. Al Basit, The Expander

Al Qabid, Al Basit, Ya Shakur

This heart contracts
and expands to encompass You,
who encompass all things,
and every Name.
First must come the emptying,
before we can fill with You;
La ilaha
il Allah.
And yet that very emptying
is also of You—
no place,
no time,
no marker remaining
in the Vastness
of the Unseen, breathing-out
of all existence,
in a moment of release.
And with a pause
between the worlds,
the breath returns,
a tide of being rushing
in to be known,
filling
all the canyons,
riverbeds, and lakes
holding the waters of Your Love
within this subtle frame
that waits
to catch another glimpse
of Your Beloved Names

dancing in the Light
of an awakened heart and mind,
which we might be,
through the gift of Your Grace.
Ya Qabid, Ya Basit,
O You who continually bring us near,
and breathe us out with Your Love,
with every beat of our hearts.
May it be that our eye,
also, does not swerve,
even as the Prophet's,
whether compressed in sadness
or expanded with joy,
may we know Your Presence
in all ways
and give thanks.
Subhanallah,
for You are subtle
in Your giving.
Do not let us fail to recognize
Your gift, no matter
how it may be wrapped.
And give to God a goodly loan.
"Arise, O enfolded one!"
We give thanks to You,
Ya Shakur,
O Creator of All Thankfulness,
for the gift of gratitude.

Al Qabid, The One Who Constricts, Bringing Us Near,
Al Basit, The One Who Expands Our Hearts,
Ya Shakur, O Creator of All Thankfulness,
You Who Are Responsive to Gratitude,
Subhanallah, Glory be to God!

*Have We not expanded your chest, and removed from you the burden
which weighed down your back, and increased your remembrance?
So, truly, with every difficulty comes ease;
truly, with every difficulty comes ease.
So when you are free from your task continue to strive,
and to your Sustainer turn with loving attention.*
[94:1–8]

*For indeed he saw Him/Her a second time
near the Lote-tree beyond which none may pass,
near which is the Garden of Promise.
Behold, the Lote-tree was veiled in a veil of nameless splendor;
his eye never wavered nor did it stray!
For, truly did he see the finest signs of his Sustainer!*
[53:13–18]

*Who is it that will offer up unto God a goodly loan,
which He/She will amply repay, with manifold increase?
For God takes away, and He/She gives abundantly;
and it is unto Him/Her that you will all be brought back.*
[2:245]

*And God said: "Behold, I shall be with you!
If you are constant in prayer, and spend in charity,
and have faith in My messengers and aid them,
and offer up unto God a goodly loan,
I will surely efface your ill deeds
and bring you into gardens through which running waters flow."*
[5:12]

*Arise, O enfolded one! And Your Sustainer's greatness glorify,
and your inner self purify!*
[74:1–4]

"Truly, the hearts of all the children of Adam
are between the two fingers,

out of the fingers of the Compassionate Lord,
as one heart.
He turns that to any direction He pleases.
O Allah, the Turner of hearts, turn our hearts to Your obedience."
[*Hadith* of the Prophet Muhammad]

"Neither the heavens nor the earth can contain Me;
only the heart of My faithful servant can contain Me."
[*Hadith Qudsi*]

22. Al Khafid, The One Who Brings Low
& 23. Ar Rafi, The Exalter

Al Khafid, Ar Rafi, Ya Wadud, Al Karim

O You who bring us low,
that You might exalt us within You—
when we are exalted in this world,
there is a danger—
our self-consciousness may increase,
and we may lose
the palpable sense of Your Presence
that inundates us
when we are near,
bowing in prostration
before Your Face.
Sometimes we need
humiliation
to find You,
who have never left us—
it is only we who may have left You,
but only ever for a moment,
for with each breath
we are returned—
though our minds
may not yet perceive it.
Your Graciousness is so vast,
You would never turn away—
You who are the very fabric of our being,
the pulsing of our day
and night,
bright with Your Loving,
through the stars
that light our way—
Your friends are always smiling

for they know the secret
of Your Ever-Present Joy
that exalts us,
from even the darkest space
we may traverse,
ringing, resounding with Your Names
dancing in our hearts,
throughout eternity.
Every morning we are Home.
Ya Khafid, Ar Rafi,
Ya Wadud, Al Karim.

Ya Khafid, O You Who Bring Low, *Ar Rafi*, The Exalter,
Ya Wadud, O You Who Are So Completely Loving,
Al Karim, The Infinitely Generous

By the fig and the olive,
and Mount Sinai,
and this city of security,[19]
truly, We have created human beings in the most beautiful proportion.
Then We reduce them to the lowest of the low
except those who have faith and act rightly:
for they shall have an unceasing reward.
Then what after this can turn you away from this Way?
Is not God the Wisest of Judges?
[95:1–8]

O you who have attained to faith!
When you are told, "Make space for one another in your gatherings,"
do make space: God will make space for you.
And whenever you are told, "Rise up," arise—

---

19 The fig, and the olive, Mount Sinai and the City of Security (Mecca) are representative of the major prophets of the Abrahamic tradition and also the aspects of the human being that have the capacity to receive revelation.

God will exalt by degrees those among you who have come to tranquility in faith,
those who have been entrusted with inner knowing—
for God is fully aware of all that you do.
[58:11]

We do raise by degrees whom We will.
Truly, your Sustainer is All Wise, All Knowing.
And We bestowed on [Abraham] Isaac and Jacob;
and We guided each of them as We had guided Noah.
And out of his offspring, David, and Solomon, and Job,
and Joseph, and Moses, and Aaron:
for thus do We reward the doers of good;
and Zachariah, and John, and Jesus, and Elijah—
every one of them was of the righteous;
and Ishmael, and Elisha, and Jonah, and Lot.
Upon all of them We bestowed graces for the sake of the worlds,
and some of their forefathers and their offspring and their siblings—
We chose them, and guided them to a straight way.
Such is God's guidance: He/She gives that guidance
to whom He/She pleases of His/Her servants.
[6:83–88]

He/She is the One who causes the dawn to break;
and He/She has made the night to be a source of stillness,
and the sun and the moon for reckoning
by the order of the Almighty, the All Knowing.
And He/She it is who has made the stars for you
so that you might be guided by them
through the darknesses of land and sea:
clearly have We detailed Our signs for people of inner knowing.
[6:96–97]

"My companions are like stars;
whichever among them you follow you will be rightly guided."
[*Hadith* of the Prophet Muhammad]

24. Al Muʿizz, The One Who Bestows Honor
& 25. Al Mudhill, The One Who Humbles

Ya Muʿizz, Al Mudhill, Ya ʿAlim, Ya Wadud

You exalt us
to the stars
that we might know
humility
before Your Power
and Your Beauty.
Before the glory
of Your Beingness,
encompassing
and breathing
through these hearts,
and every smallest particle
of earthliness
and stars
so far beyond our sight,
we weep
and kneel.
Mudhill—
we are but a mud-hill
in comparison
to Your Capacity
for Creation,
for Enlivening,
and yet,
this lump of clay
can speak,
and can hear Your Voice
so intimately
within each cell
as it is awakened

to the Power of Your Love
that calls us all
into Glory
and raises us
up in Your Heart
of hearts—
You Who do us the Honor
of calling our name
and bringing us
close to You,
even while still
in this frame
of watery earth,
inspired
by Your Knowing
and Your Breath.
O Hidden Treasure
within everything
that is, whose Truth
becomes more and more
manifest
for eyes
that begin to see,
Ya Mudhill,
Ya Mu'izz,
we honor and praise You
who have Loved
us all
into being.
Subhanallah,
Ya Rabb al Alameen.

Ya Mu'izz, O You Who Raise us High in Honor,
Al Mudhill, The One Who Humbles as Is Needed
(that We Might Know Your Face Within),

Ya 'Alim, O You Who Know All
(That Which Is Manifest and That Which Is Hidden),
Ya Wadud, O You Who Love So Infinitely,
Subhanallah! Ya Rabb al Alameen, Glory be to You, Sustainer of All Worlds

Say: "O God, Sovereign of all dominion!
You grant dominion unto whom You will,
and take away dominion from whom You will;
and You raise up whom You will, and bring low whom You will.
In Your Hand is all good.
Truly, You have the power to will anything.
[3:26]

Hasn't the time come for the faithful
that their hearts in all humility
should engage in the remembrance of God
and of all the Truth that has been revealed?
[57:16]

Don't you see how God has created the seven heavens in harmony
and made the moon a light in their midst
and made the sun a glorious lamp?
And how God has caused you to grow gradually from the earth,
and in the end He/She will return you to it
and then raise you forth anew?
And God has unfolded wide the earth for you
that you might move about there on spacious paths.
[71:15–20]

God, unto whom there are many ways of ascent:
all the angels and all the inspiration granted ascend unto Him/Her
in a day the length of which is akin to fifty thousand years . . . .
And so endure all adversity with goodly patience.
Behold, people look upon that as something far away—
but We see it as near!
[70:3–7]

"I was a Hidden Treasure and I so loved to be known
that I created the worlds, seen and Unseen,
in order that My Treasure of Generosity and Loving-kindness
might be known."
[*Hadith Qudsi*]

*Those who were conscious of their Sustainer will be urged on in throngs
towards the Garden until, when they reach it,
they shall find its gates wide-open;
and its keepers will say unto them,
"Peace be upon you! Well have you done:
enter, then, herein to continually abide!"
And they will exclaim: "All praise is due to God,
who has made His promise to us come true,
and has bestowed upon us this expanse as our inheritance,
so that we may dwell in the Garden as we please!"
And how excellent a reward will it be for those who labored!
And you will see the angels surrounding the Throne of Almightiness,
celebrating their Sustainer's glory and praise.
And judgment will have been passed in justice on all, and it will be said:
"All praise belongs to God, the Sustainer of all the worlds!"*
[39:73–75]

*And see; and in time they, too, will come to see.
Limitless in His/Her glory is your Sustainer, the Sustainer of Nobility—
far beyond anything by which they may attempt to define Him/Her!
And peace be with all the Messengers!
And all praise belongs to God alone, the Sustainer of all the Worlds.*
[37:179–182]

26. As Sami, The All Hearing One

Ya Sami, Ya Basir

Ahh! The moon is full!
No wonder I can't sleep.
Thank You
for bringing me
out
into its radiance.
The cicadas drone in celebration,
and tree frogs "ribbit" in response.
Vibration pulses
everywhere,
in light,
in sound,
in hearts.
This week I learned
it really matters
who tunes your piano,
what they are hearing,
and how their heart is tuned.
Overtones linger
of our own narratives
we have whispered.
What is the story
we are telling ourselves?
Is it Yours,
O You who hear all things
and know
when we are out of tune?
Rectify us in Your truest sound.
Realign our voices
and all our corresponding movements
into praise,

into songs of celebration,
of service, and of love!
Ahh! Lady, sweet Lady
who listened so well,
you brought forth new being
within such radiance—
the sound of the Beloved,
whispered through an angel,
became a blessed son
whose word opened hearts
and still does.
May we, also, listen with such care
to the songs
that You are singing
in our lives,
in our deepest hearts,
O Sami, You Who Are All Hearing,
the Most Beautiful Sound of all sounds.

Ya Sami, O You Who Are All Hearing,
Ya Basir, O You Who Are All Seeing

Remain conscious of God: for, truly, God is All Hearing, All Knowing!
[49:1]

And when Abraham and Ishmael were raising the foundations of the Temple,
[they prayed:] "O our Sustainer! Accept this from us:
for, truly, You alone are All Hearing, All Knowing!
O our Sustainer! Bring our selves into surrender to You,
and make of our offspring a community that shall surrender itself to You,
and show us our ways of worship, and accept our repentance:
for, truly, You alone are the Acceptor of Repentance, the Infinitely Merciful!"
[2:127–128]

*These are messages of a Book
clear in itself and clearly showing the truth.
We convey to you some of the story of Moses and Pharaoh,
setting forth the truth for people who will have faith.*
[28:1–3]

*Limitless in His/Her glory
is He/She who transported His/Her servant by night
from the Inviolable House of Worship [in Mecca]
to the Remote House of Worship [in Jerusalem]—
the environs of which We had blessed—
so that We might show him some of Our signs:
for, truly, He/She alone is All Hearing, All Seeing.
And even so We entrusted revelation unto Moses,
and made it a guidance for the children of Israel.*
[17:1–2]

*Lo! The angels said: "O Mary! Behold,
God sends you the glad tiding, through a word from Him,
[of a son] who shall become known as the Christ Jesus,
son of Mary, of great honor in this world
and in the life to come, and of those who are drawn near to God.*
[3:45]

*Always remember the blessings which God has bestowed on you,
and the solemn pledge by which He/She bound you to Himself/Herself
when you said, "We have heard, and we pay heed."
And so, remain conscious of God:
truly, God has full knowledge of what is within hearts.*
[5:7]

*With Him/Her are the secrets of the heavens and the earth:
how clearly He/She sees; how finely He/She hears!*
[18:26]

> O You who dwell in the gardens,
> the companions hearken to Your voice:
> cause me to hear it.
> [The Bible, Song of Solomon, 8:13]

27. Al Basir, The All Seeing

Ya Basir, Ya Nur

Ya Basir!
Every morning You open our eyes
with the capacity to see,
to find You.
The leaves clap their hands
with Your breeze of Joy
that heralds the sun's rise.
The Light with which You grace us
inundates our hearts,
and we leap up whirling
to catch sight of You,
to our right
and to our left.
There is no inch of this Creation
that is without You.
What a mirror
You hold before us!
What a mirror You make of us,
when *we keep seeking Your Face,*
mornings and evenings.
Even through the darkness
we can find Your Path—
turning to the heavens,
we watch the stars,
and You lead us
step by heartbeat by Love.
Sometimes those
whose eyes seem dim
see more deeply.
Inner, outer,
which is better?

Each serves a purpose,
and that purpose is You—
praise and service
of the One
Who Encompasses All Vision
far beyond our sight,
The One,
The All Knowing,
The Truth.

Ya Basir, O You Who Are All Seeing, Who Encompass All Vision,
Ya Nur, O Light, *Al Ahad*, The One,
Al 'Alim, The All Knowing,
Al Haqq, The Truth

"O God allow us to see the truth as the truth,
and give us the blessing of following it."
[*Hadith* of the Prophet Muhammad]

Look around you!
In the creation of the heavens and the earth;
in the alternation of night and day;
in the sailing of ships through the ocean for the profit of humankind;
in the waters which God sends down from the skies
and the life which the One gives by means of it to an earth that is dead;
in the living creatures of all kinds which multiply there;
in the change of the winds
and the clouds that follow, between sky and earth;
truly, these are signs for people who reflect.
[2:164]

With Him/Her are the secrets of the heavens and the earth:
how clearly He/She sees; how finely He/She hears!
They have no protector other than Him/Her;
nor does He/She share His/Her Command with anyone.

And speak what has been revealed to you of the Book of your Lord:
nothing can change His/Her Words,
and you will find no refuge other than Him/Her.
And keep your soul content with those
who call on their Sustainer morning and evening seeking His/Her Face.
[18:26–28]

Earlier, We gave Moses guidance,
and We gave the Book as an inheritance to the children of Israel—
a guide and a reminder to people of insight.
So patiently persevere, for God's promise is true;
and ask forgiveness for your mistakes
and celebrate the praises of your Sustainer—
in the evening and in the morning.
[40:53–55]

Such is God, your Sustainer: there is no god but Hu,
the Creator of everything: then worship Him/Her alone—
for it is He/She who has everything in His/Her care.
No vision can encompass Him/Her,
but He/She encompasses all vision:
for He/She alone is Subtle Beyond Comprehension, All Aware.
[6:102–3]

28. Al Hakam, The Judge

Al Hakam, Ya Nur, Ya Rahim, Ya Salaam

O Most Dear Judge,
You who care for every aspect of our being,
why can't we turn to You
when we have a question?
For surely, You have told us,
I will answer.
If we listen to Your Word,
and follow those with light
upon their brow,
from deep within the heart
of openings to Your chambers,
our lives might gain Your Splendor
Your Generous Heart of hearts,
Your Merciful manner
of balancing the right from the wrong.
"O Lord, make it easy, don't make it difficult."
Such beauty is all around us,
if only we would look,
and read Your Name
in our own book.
Judgment comes
as a delight to our hearts,
for You would have us be near;
Your rectifying touch
can wipe the past away,
as we stand together on the plain
of transcendence
and know the realms
of Your expansive breath
that would open our hearts
from constriction.

Prison doors fly open;
You long ago
gave us the key,
and have only been waiting
for us to say, "Yes,"
we truly wish to be free.
You wrap us in new clothes
of the most beautiful array
and pour rivers of blessing
beneath our feet,
in the Garden,
where the birds are always singing,
and there is peace.

Al Hakam, The Best Judge,
Ya Nur, O Light,
Ya Rahim, O Infinitely Merciful One,
Ya Salaam, O You Who Are Peace

Judgment rests with none but God.
He/She shall declare the truth,
since it is He/She who is the Best Judge between truth and falsehood.
[6:57]

Call upon Me; I will answer.
[40:60]

Follow the way of those who turn to Me:
in the end you will all return to Me,
and I will make clear to you the truth
of all that you were doing.
[31:15]

A book We have revealed to you
so that you might bring forth all humankind,

by their Sustainer's blessing, out of the depths of darkness into the light:
onto the way of the Almighty, the One to whom all praise belongs.
[14:1]

Consider the sun and its splendor, and the moon as she follows.
Consider the day as it reveals this world,
and the night as it conceals it.
Consider the scope of the heavens and its wondrous structure;
consider the earth and its broad expanse.
Consider the soul and the order and proportion given to it,
and its enlightenment as to that which is wrong and right:
truly, the one who purifies it shall reach a happy state.
[91:1–9]

"O Lord, make it easy, don't make it difficult."
[*Hadith* of the Prophet Muhammad]

Who is as the wise man?
And who knows the interpretation of a thing?
A man's wisdom makes his face shine,
and the boldness of his face shall be changed.
[The Bible, Ecclesiastes, 8:1]

Anyone—be it man or woman—who does good deeds
and is of the faithful, shall enter the Garden,
and shall not be wronged by as much as the groove on the pit of a date.
And who could be of better faith
than the one who surrenders his or her whole being to God
and is a doer of good,
and follows the Way of Abraham, the true in faith—
seeing that God chose Abraham for a beloved friend?
For, to God belongs all that is in the heavens and on earth;
and indeed God encompasses all things.
[4:124–126]

*Those who have attained to faith and do righteous deeds—
and We do not burden any soul with more than it is well able to bear—
they will be companions of the Garden, there to dwell,
after We shall have removed whatever unworthy thoughts or feelings
may have been lingering in their hearts.
Running waters will flow at their feet;
and they will say: "All praise belongs to God, Who has guided us here;
for certainly we would not have found the right path
unless God were our guide!
Truly, our Sustainer's messengers have told us the truth!"
And a voice will call out to them:
"This is the Garden which by virtue of your deeds has come to you."*
[7:42–43]

29. Al 'Adl, The Most Just

Ya 'Adl, Ya Hakam, Ya Hadi, Ya Salaam

If they argue with you,
say, "God knows best
what it is you are doing."
God will judge—
between you
when the Day dawns.
And you, too, will see
where you have been
all these moments
of your breath
upon the winds
of your desires.
O Hadi,
clear our vision
now.
Let us rule
with Your Justice
these selves,
that they might serve
a greater wholeness
of all these hearts
yearning
for Your Love.
In each other,
through each other,
through the Garden
and its greening rivers,
may we find our Source.
"Will you come
to this rendezvous?"
You are always asking.

The balance is ready
to weigh these hearts of light
and the songs
we have been singing.
The Word of your Lord
finds its fulfillment
in truth and justice.
No one can change His/Her words:
for He/She is the One
Who Hears and Knows
all things.
Forever Your Word
resounds,
O You who hear
all tongues speaking
and discern the Truth
of all we are creating.
From the Truth,
to the Truth—
Your inspiration
keeps this world afloat—
that inner Truth—
may it crack open
the shell of our opinions,
that the seeds
You have planted
might fall into Your arms,
and ripen,
face to Face
with Your Beauty.
The human spirit
so longs for freedom—
for those who are patient
and do the deeds of wholeness
and reconciliation
is forgiveness:

*"Peace;
enter thou My Garden."*

Ya 'Adl, O Most Just,
Ya Hakam, O Judge,
Ya Hadi, O Guide,
Ya Salaam, O You Who Are Peace

*To every community We have appointed ways of worship,
which they ought to observe.
And so, do not let others draw you into arguing about it,
but invite them to your Sustainer:
for you are indeed on the right way.
And if they argue with you, say: "God knows best what you are doing."
Indeed, God will judge between you on the Day of Resurrection
concerning everything about which you would differ.*
[22:67–69]

*O you who have attained to faith! Stand firmly in your devotion to God,
bearing witness to the truth in complete fairness; and never let hatred of anyone
lead you to make the mistake of deviating from justice.
Be just: this is closest to being God-conscious.
And remain conscious of God: truly, God is well-aware of all that you do.*
[5:8]

*The Word of your Lord finds its fulfillment in truth and in justice.
No one can change His/Her words:
for He/She is the One Who Hears and Knows all things.*
[6:115]

*See: truly, with those close to God
there is no fear nor shall they grieve;
those who have faith and constantly guard against harm,
for them are glad tidings in the present life and in the life to come:*

no alteration can there be in the Words of God.
This is indeed the ultimate prosperity.
[10:62–64]

He/She has created the heavens and the earth in accordance with Truth,
and He/She shaped you and made your shapes beautiful;
and with Him/Her is your journey's return.
[64:3]

And never call upon any other deity side by side with God.
There is no deity but Hu.
Everything is perishing, except His/Her Face.
With Him/Her rests all judgment:
and to Him/Her shall you all return.
[28:88]

Those who attain to faith and do righteous deeds
We shall bring into gardens through which running waters flow,
therein to abide beyond the count of time;
there shall they have spouses pure
and We shall bring them into sheltered happiness.
Behold, God bids you to deliver
all that with which you have been entrusted
unto those who are entitled thereto,
and whenever you judge between people, to judge with justice.
Truly, most excellent is what God counsels you to do:
truly, God is All Hearing, All Seeing!
[4:57–58]

Those who patiently persevere
and do the deeds of wholeness and reconciliation—
for them is forgiveness and a great reward.
[11:11]

"Peace; enter thou My Garden."
[36:58; 36:26]

30. Al Latif, The Infinitely Subtle One

Ya Latif, Ya Khabir, Ya Nur

Beloved One,
heal our ills—
each one of us
has a journey
toward greater health
with You.
Listening deeply
to Your songs—
vibration redirects;
our neuropathways realign.
Empty of our own recordings
we turn afresh
to the silence
that holds all sound,
and wait
for Your whales and dolphins
to share their chants
from underwater realms
in the vast Sea
of Your Being.
Beloved friends gather
in the sunshine
by the shore,
where air meets water
and earth
and Your messages arrive
with the tides
within our hearts—
we smile,
enlivened
by Your sweet radiance,

Ya Latif, Ya Khabir,
Ya Sami, Ya Basir,
Ya Quddus,
Ya Nur
al samawati wal ard,
and *truly this*
is a message
for all the worlds.
Inner and outer
dance in Your Love,
O Most Subtle of Mysteries,
Ya Latif, Ya Wadud.

Ya Latif, O Most Mysteriously Subtle in Presence and Gently Kind,
Ya Khabir, O All Aware,
Ya Sami, O All Hearing One, *Ya Basir*, O All Seeing One,
Ya Quddus, O Most Holy and Pure,
Ya Nur al samawati wal ard, O Light of the heavens and the earth,
Ya Wadud, O Infinitely Loving One

And whether you hide your word or declare it,
He/She certainly knows the secrets of hearts.
Should He/She not know, He/She who created?
And He/She is the Most Subtle, and the One Who is Aware of Everything.
[67:13–14]

Truly, my Sustainer is Subtle Beyond Comprehension in whatever He/She wills:
truly, He/She alone is All Knowing, Truly Wise!
[12:100]

"O my dear son, truly, though there be anything
of but the weight of a mustard-seed,
and though it be hidden in a rock, or in the skies, or in the earth,
God will bring it to light:
for, behold, God is Subtle in Mystery, All Aware.

*O my dear son! Be constant in prayer, and enjoin the doing of what is right
and forbid the doing of what is wrong,
and bear in patience whatever may befall you:
this, behold, is something upon which to set one's heart!"*
[31:16–17, prayer of the Prophet Luqman]

*Say: "I follow what is revealed to me by my Sustainer—
this revelation is a means of insight from your Sustainer,
and a guidance and grace to those who will have faith.
And so when the Quran is voiced, pay attention,
and listen in silence, so that you might be graced with God's mercy."
And remember your Sustainer humbly within yourself and with awe,
and without raising your voice, in the morning and in the evening;
and don't allow yourself to be unaware.*
[7:203–205]

*God alone is the Most High, the Most Great!
Aren't you aware how the ships speed through the sea by God's favor,
so that He/She might show you some of His/Her wonders?
Herein, behold, there are messages indeed
for all who are wholly patient in adversity and deeply grateful.*
[31:30–31]

God is the Light of the heavens and the earth.
[24:35]

*This is no less than a reminder to all the worlds.
And after a while you will know its meaning.*
[38:87–88]

To everything there is a season,
and a time to every purpose under heaven.
[The Bible, Ecclesiastes, 3:1]

31. Al Khabir, The All Aware

Ya Khabir, Ya Nur, Ya Latif, Ya Rahim

Your Name is written
on the clouds
in script
we are only
just beginning to decipher.
Water above,
water below,
shining in the Light,
held in water
before our birth,
we cry
when we are forced
to land.
You are aware
of our need,
and give us breath
to ask,
pouring Your Awareness
through us
until we understand
that You
are our true sustenance.
So subtly
You intimate
our need to us,
until we hear
our cells crying—
thirsting
for the water
of Your springs,
and rose windows

open.
The light of our eyes
is birthed by Your command,
and trees grow
through our limbs
lit with Your oil—
of an olive
neither of the east
nor of the west,
for You are beyond
sunrise
and sunset—
You are Al Khabir,
and *in Heaven is our provision.*

Ya Khabir, O You who Are All Aware,
Ya Nur, O Light,
Ya Latif, O Most Subtle in Mystery and Nobility,
Ya Rahim, O Infinitely Merciful

God is He/She except whom there is no deity:
the One who knows all that is beyond the reach of a created being's perception,
as well as all that can be witnessed by a creature's senses or mind:
He/She, the Infinitely Compassionate, the Infinitely Merciful.
[59:22]

In whatever business you may be engaged,
whatever portion of the Quran you may be reciting,
whatever deed you may be doing,
We are Witnesses of it when you are immersed in it.
For not even the weight of an atom on the earth or in heaven
is beyond the awareness of Your Sustainer.
And there is neither the least nor the greatest of these things but are clearly recorded.
See: truly, with the friends of God there is no fear nor shall they grieve.
[10:61–62]

And remember all that is recited in your homes of God's signs and wisdom:
for God is Subtly Mysterious, All Aware.
[33:34]

He/She knows all that is beyond the reach of a created being's perception,
as well as all that can be witnessed:
for He/She alone is Truly Wise, All Aware.
[6:73]

He/She bestows from on high in due measure, as He/She wills:
for, truly, He/She is fully aware of [the needs of] His/Her servants, and sees them all.
And it is He/She who sends down rain
after they have lost all hope, unfolding His/Her Mercy:
for He/She alone is the Protector, the One to Whom All Praise Belongs.
[42:27–28]

God is the Light of the heavens and the earth.
The parable of His/Her light is,
as it were, that of a niche containing a lamp;
the lamp is enclosed in glass, the glass like a radiant star;
lit from a blessed tree—an olive-tree
that is neither of the east nor of the west—
the oil of which would almost give light
even though fire had not touched it: light upon light!
God guides to His/Her light the one who wills to be guided;
and God offers parables to human beings,
since God has full knowledge of all things.
[24:35]

In Heaven is your provision.
[51:22]

32. Al Halim, The Most Forbearing

Ya Halim, Ya Karim

O Most Forbearing One,
You Who Are Most Generous
in Your Forgiveness
and Patient in
Your Kindness
when we forget—
You envision
our wholeness
and awareness
and forgive us
for our transgressions
and our blindness,
standing firm
in Your Forbearance,
holding us all
in Your Love
that we might not fall
far
from the orbits
You project
and guide,
of all the planets—
heaven and earth
are under Your sway—
we swing
through night and day,
and always
You are listening,
watching,
knowing
the unfolding

of our wings
and bringing us
into the realms
of Your Beauty
where we are well-pleased.
Subhanallah!
Glory be to You,
All Knowing,
Ever-Forbearing,
Infinitely Generous,
and Oft Forgiving One,
Most Patient, Most Kind,
Restorer of Peace
in our hearts,
in our minds,
in every cell
that awakens
again and again
to Your Love.

Ya Halim, O Most Forbearing One,
Ya Karim, O Infinitely Generous One,
Subhanallah! Glory be to God!
Ya 'Alim, O All Knowing One,
Ya Ghafur, O Oft Forgiving One,
Ya Sabur, O Infinitely Patient One,
Ya Rauf, O Most Kind,
Ya Mu'id, O Restorer,
Ya Salaam, O You Who Are Peace,
Ya Wadud, O Infinite Love

*Truly, it is God who upholds the celestial bodies and the earth,
lest they deviate [from their orbits]—*

for if they should ever deviate, there is none who could uphold them afterwards.
Truly, He/She is Most Forbearing, Oft Forgiving!
[35:41]

And among His/Her wonders is your sleep, at night or in daytime,
as well as your quest of some of His/Her bounties:
in this, behold, there are messages indeed for people who listen!
[30:23]

As for those who avoid the grave sins and shameful deeds,
though occasionally they may stumble—
truly, your Sustainer is Vast in Forgiveness.
He/She knows you well when He/She brings you out of the earth
and when you are hidden in your mother's wombs;
so do not claim purity for yourselves—
He/She knows best who is conscious of Him/Her.
[53:32]

Remain, then, conscious of God as best you can, and listen and pay heed.
And spend in charity for the good of your own selves:
for such as from their own covetousness are saved—
it is they, they who shall attain to a happy state!
If you offer up to God a goodly loan, He/She will amply repay you for it,
and will forgive you your sins:
for God is Ever Responsive to Gratitude, Most Forbearing,
knowing all that is beyond the reach of a created being's perception
as well as all that can be witnessed by a creature's senses or mind—
the Almighty, the Most Wise!
[64:16–18]

The seven heavens acclaim His/Her limitless glory,
and the earth, and all that they contain;
and there is not a single thing but celebrates His/Her limitless glory and praise:
but you fail to grasp the manner of their glorifying Him/Her!
Truly, He/She is Most Forbearing, Oft Forgiving!
[17:44]

God will most certainly provide for them a goodly sustenance: for, truly, God—
He/She alone—is the Best of Providers;
He/She will most certainly cause them to enter
upon a state with which they shall be well-pleased:
for, truly, God is All Knowing, Most Forbearing.
Thus shall it be.
[22:58–60]

33. Al 'Azim, The Most Magnificent

Al 'Azim, Ya 'Aziz, Ya Hakim, Ya Wadud

Every day there is a choice—
in which direction do we turn?
To magnify Your Glory,
or our own supposed name—
when we have forgotten
how You have called us
from before the before—
O You Who Are Mighty,
Most Magnificent,
we are turned
to the right and the left,
even as the sun rises
and the sun sets,
between the fingers
of Your Hand of Power
that keeps us moving
in the pattern of Your Love,
despite the wobbles of our orbits
and the misalignment of our choice.
In any moment we can listen,
we can awaken
to a greater whole,
O Wisest of the Wise,
until the Vastness
of Your Majesty
grabs our hearts
and will not let go.
Ya 'Aziz,
You Who Are So Mighty
in the Power of Your Love,
these feeble words

fall in petals at your feet—
as though anyone
could stand long
in the wind of Your Compassion
that brings all the flowers Home,
returning these bodies to the earth
and these hearts
on the wings of Your Love
to the Throne of Your Magnificence
where angels gather in throngs,
and we all disappear
eye to Eye,
enveloped
by Your Heart.
Ya 'Azim,
Ya 'Aziz, Al Hakim,
Ya Rahman, Ya Wadud.

Ya 'Azim, O Most Magnificent,
Ya 'Aziz, O Most Mighty, *Al Hakim*, Wisest of the Wise,
Ya Rahman, O Infinitely Compassionate One,
Ya Wadud, O All-Loving One.

*Their shadows turn right and left,
prostrating themselves before God and utterly submissive.
For before God prostrates itself all that is in the heavens and all that is on earth—
every beast that moves, and the angels.*
[16:48–49]

*Whoever chooses to follow the right path,
follows it but for his or her own good;
and whoever goes astray, goes but astray to his or her own hurt;
and no bearer of burdens shall be made to bear another's burden.*
[17:15]

In this way does God, the Most Mighty, the Most Wise,
send inspiration to you, as to those who came before you:
to Him / Her belongs all that is in the heavens and all that is on earth;
He / She is the Most High, the Most Magnificent.
The highest heavens are well-nigh split apart in awe;
and the angels celebrate their Sustainer's limitless glory and praise,
and ask forgiveness for all who are on earth.
See, truly, God alone is Oft Forgiving, Most Merciful!
[42:3–5]

All praise is God's, the Sustainer of all worlds,
the Infinitely Compassionate and Infinitely Merciful,
Sovereign of the Day of Reckoning.
[1:2–4]

O humankind! A manifestation of the truth has now come to you
from your Sustainer, and We have sent to you a clear light.
And as for those who have attained to faith in God and hold fast to Him / Her—
He / She will cause them to enter into His / Her Compassion
and His / Her abundant blessing,
and guide them to Himself / Herself by a straight way.
[4:174–5]

Truly, your Sustainer is indeed Infinitely Compassionate, Infinitely Merciful.
[16:7]

Say: "God is enough for me!
There is no god but Him / Her. In Him / Her have I placed my trust,
for He / She is the Sustainer, in Awe-Inspiring Almightiness enthroned."
[9:129]

It is He / She who from on high has bestowed inner peace
upon the hearts of the faithful,
so that—seeing that God's are all the forces of the heavens and the earth,
and that God is All Knowing, Most Wise Healer of the Wise—
they might grow yet more firm in their faith,

*that He/She might admit the faithful, both men and women,
into gardens through which running waters flow, there to abide,
and that He/She might erase their ill deeds—
and that is, in the sight of God, indeed a triumph supreme!*
[48:4–5]

35. Ash-Shakur, The Grateful, Ever Responsive to Gratitude

Ya Shakur, Ya Wahhab, Ya Wadud, Ya Karim

We give thanks
to You,
the Creator of All Gratitude,
for instilling these hearts
with a Way
toward Your Abundance
and Ever-present Grace.
So often,
You give us cause
to be grateful—
for our health,
for loved ones,
precious in our remembrance,
nurtured by Your Sustenance,
for all the beauties
that surround us
in the birds, and trees, and streams,
the graceful hills
and caverns deep with gems
that sparkle with Your Light,
igniting the fire of appreciation
in our souls
for all the blessings
of this life
and the Nearness
to which You draw us
with the magnetism
of Your Love
that renders
all our complaints

helpless
before the Power
of Your Giving,
Ya Wahhab,
Ya Wadud, Ya Karim.
Forever, we sing Your praise,
Ya Shakur,
You Who inundate these hearts
with waves of thankfulness,
turning us
inside out,
to know Your Name
in all its facets
and to sing,
"Glory be to God!"

Ya Shakur, O Creator of All Thankfulness, Ever Responsive to Gratitude,
    Ya Wahhab, O You Who Overcome Us with Your Infinite Giving,
Ya Wadud, O Infinitely Loving One, *Ya Karim*, O Infinitely Generous One

Those among His/Her Servants who have knowledge
stand in awe of God:
for God is Almighty, Oft Forgiving.
Those who remember the Book of God and are constant in prayer,
and distribute out of what We have provided for them,
secretly and openly, hope for an exchange that will never fail:
for He/She will pay them their due,
no, He/She will give them even more out of His/Her abundance;
for He/She is Oft Forgiving, Always Responsive to Gratitude.
[35:28–30]

"All praise is due to God, who has caused all sorrow to leave us:
for, truly, our Sustainer is indeed Oft Forgiving,
Ever Responsive to Gratitude."
[35:34]

*Say [O Prophet]: "No reward do I ask of you for this
other than loving those who are near.
For if anyone gains a good deed,
We shall grant him or her through it an increase of good:
and, truly, God is Oft Forgiving, Ever Responsive to Gratitude.*
[42:23]

*And thus do We give many facets to Our signs,
so that they might say, "You have been taught well,"
and that We might make it clear to people of inner knowing;
follow what has been revealed to you by your Sustainer.
There is no God but He/She.*
[6:105–106]

*We bestowed this wisdom on Luqman:
"Be grateful to God."
Anyone who is grateful does so to the profit of his or her own soul.*
[31:12]

"Thankfulness and gratitude is the way of the prophet."
[~ Mevlana Jalaluddin Rumi, *The Mathnawi*, VI:1829]

36. Al 'Ali, The Most High

Ya 'Ali, Ya Muta'ali

We love to love You,
Ya 'Ali, Ya Muta'ali,
for You lift our spirits
from within Your Self
to Yourself—
the highest vantage point
is Yours to give,
and so You bestow it,
upon Your servants—
those who understand
that in bowing low they are exalted;
face to Face in prostration
our hearts instinctively call,
"Subhana Rabbiyal 'Ala,"[20]
and again we acknowledge,
"Subhana Rabbiyal 'Ala."
In resonance we are entrained
by heart to know You,
O Subtlest of the subtle
vapor of Love that moves
in the Most Magnificent speed
to raise our station
as You choose—
You who give us will
in order to respond
from our own knowing instilled

---

20 *Subhana Rabbiyal 'Ala*: "Glory be to my Lord, the Most High": this phrase is spoken three times internally with each prostration of prayer of the salah. It is in prostration that we make our *miraj* (our ascension, following the example of the Prophet Muhammad into the Presence of the Most High).

by You
in every cell that seeks its highest
functioning
in order and in balance.
We see You
because You have seen us
long before our existence,
and beside the Throne
we have declared, "Yes,
You are my Lord,"
and we stand in rectitude
on the path of Your service
that leads us with the stars
to shine in Your Brilliance,
O Allah,
You who are our very essence,
Ya 'Ali, Ya Muta'ali,
Ya Nur, Ya Rahim,
Ya Haqq al Arsh al 'Azim,
Ya Latif, Ya Wadud!

Ya 'Ali, O Most Sublimely High,
Ya Muta'ali, O Most Exalted Essence,
Ya Nur, O You Who Are Light, *Ya Rahim*, O Infinitely Merciful,
Ya Haqq al Arsh al 'Azim, O Truth of the Most Magnificent Throne,
Ya Latif, O Most Subtle and Kind, *Ya Wadud*, O Love

He/She knows all that is beyond the reach of a created being's perception
as well as all that can be witnessed—the Most Great,
the One Who Is Far Above Anything that is or could ever be,
the Most Exalted in Magnificence.
[13:9]

And whenever your Sustainer brings forth their offspring
from the loins of the children of Adam,

*He/She calls upon them to bear witness regarding themselves:
"Am I not your Sustainer?"—to which they answer:
"Yes, indeed, we do bear witness!"²¹*
[7:172]

*Is he not acquainted with what is in the books of Moses
and of Abraham who was true to his trust?
Namely that no bearer of burdens can bear the burden of another;
that the human being can have nothing but that for which he or she strives;
that in time his or her striving will become apparent;
and then he or she will be recompensed with the most complete recompense;
that to your Sustainer is the final Goal;
that it is He/She alone who causes your laughter and your tears;
that it is He/She who grants death and life;
that He/She created in pairs, male and female,
from a drop of sperm as it is poured forth;
and that with Him/Her rests another coming to life;
that it is He/She who gives wealth and contentment;
and that it is He/She alone who sustains the brightest star.²²*
[53:36–49]

*To Him/Her belongs all that is in the heavens and on earth:
and He/She is the Most High, the Most Great.*
[42:4]

*God—there is no deity but Hu,
the Ever Living, the Self-Subsisting Source of all Being.
No slumber can seize Him/Her nor sleep.
All things in heaven and on earth belong to Hu.*

---

21 This refers, also, to what is known as the "Day of Alast," when in pre-eternity all the spirits were gathered around God, who asked: "Am I not your Lord (*Alastu bi Rabbikum*)?" To which the faithful answered, "Yes," and are continually called to remember this trust and promised faithfulness.

22 Sirius, of the constellation Canis Major, the brightest star in the heavens. This phrase might also be understood as, "it is God alone who sustains the brightest of the saints, those who shine with His Light."

*Who could intercede in His/Her Presence
without His/Her permission?
He/She knows what appears in front of and behind His/Her creatures.
Nor can they encompass any knowledge of Him/Her
except what He/She wills.
His/Her throne extends over the heavens and the earth,
and He/She feels no fatigue in guarding and preserving them,
for He/She is the Highest and Most Exalted in Magnificence.*
[2:255]

37. Al Kabir, The Most Great

Ya Kabir, Ya Mutakabbir, Ya Wasi, Ya Wajid, Ya Basir, Ya 'Alim,
Ya Wadud, Ya Wahhab, Ya Rahim, Ya Rahman, Ya Salaam

O You who in Your Greatness
are vaster than the heavens,
whose Love enriches us
by heart
even when
we have become most desolate
and, lost in the desert
of our human devising,
have lost track
through the winds
of desire,
You find us—
always
near—
and bring us to Your side,
Ya Mutakabbir.
From the lowest
to the highest,
You encompass us with Grace,
for You are vaster
than the stars' expanse,
and earth's darkest, deepest depths.
Allahu Akbar,
You are Greater
than anything
we might imagine—
for our eyes
cannot see You;
only You can see Yourself,
inherent in all of us

and known
by that inner knowing
You bestow—
*Surely, remembrance of God
is the Greatest,*
and we know You
as You alone can help us
to know.
O Knower of all that we hold secret
and all that is manifest,
become resplendent
in our minds,
our hearts,
our lives,
for surely,
we can know
this Treasure of Your Generosity and Love,
because You have gifted us
with sensitive and subtle hearts,
Ya Wadud, Ya Wahhab,
and in that knowing,
we are restored,
returned to our origin
through Your Infinite Mercy,
to the Peace and Tranquility
of Your Infinite Compassion,
Ya Rahim,
Ya Rahman,
Ya Salaam.

Ya Kabir, O You Who Are Most Great,
Ya Mutakabbir, O Supremely Great One,
Ya Wasi, O All Encompassing One, *Ya Wajid*, O Finder,
Ya Basir, O All Seeing One, *Ya 'Alim*, O All Knowing One,
Ya Wadud, O Infinitely Loving One,
Ya Wahhab, O Overwhelming Giver of All,

Ya Rahim, O Infinitely Merciful One,
Ya Rahman, O Infinitely Compassionate,
Ya Salaam, O You Who Are Peace and Instill Peace in our hearts

*Recite what is sent of the Book by inspiration to you
and be constant in prayer:
for prayer restrains from shameful and unjust deeds,
and remembrance of God is surely the greatest.
And God knows all that you do.*
[29:45]

*With Him/Her everything is measured in accordance with its scope and purpose.
He/She knows all that is beyond the reach of a created being's perception
as well as all that can be witnessed by a creature's senses or mind—
the Great One, the One far above anything that is or could ever be!*
[13:8–9]

*Now await in patience the command of your Sustainer:
for truly you are within Our sight.
And celebrate the praises of your Sustainer
whenever you arise,
and for part of the night also praise Him/Her
and at the retreat of the stars!*
[52:48–49]

*For all those who listen to God and the Messenger
are among those on whom God has bestowed His blessings:
the prophets, and those who never deviated from the truth,
and those who with their lives bore witness to the truth,
and the righteous ones; and what a beautiful friendship this is.
Such is the abundance of God—
and it suffices that God is All Knowing.*
[4:69–70]

38. Al Hafiz, The Preserver

Ya Hafiz, Ya Hadi, Ya Hamid, Ya Samad

O You who are the Preserver,
who keep us fresh
in Your remembrance,
from long ago
You described us
and gave us
beautiful
forms
through which
to mention You
within our hearts
and sing Your Praises
from the hills,
where gentle curves
and jagged peaks
seek Your Presence
in their soil and rocks
and keep us anchored
in Your Love.
The Tablets
of Your Grace
are preserved
forever,
from before the first creation
until You inherit
all the beauties
You have poured—
this earth, the heavens,
Your Star creatures,
and these humble humans,
dolphins,

birds,
crabs,
and bees,
daffodils
and even fleas—
the gnat that
returned Nimrod
to Your knowing
and Pharaoh
in the waves of Your Red Sea,
Moses standing
on Mount Sinai
and the bush
that spoke Your Name—
he could not see you
in that moment,
until no longer Moses,
for an instant
in a swoon,
his heart
knew itself
in Your Presence
as the Tablet
Preserved,
and he could
bring
Your Revelations,
Your Guidance,
and Your Love
to parents
and children
for generations,
until Jesus, too,
inscribed
into the womb
of Mary,

poured the
wine of Your
Everlasting Love
from the Word
within his heart—
Muhammad,
the "Most Praised,"
he, too,
stood in recognition
of the Words
he heard,
Kun, fa Yakun.[23]
Forever,
You have claimed us,
that forever
we may know
we are Yours—
how could we be
other than Your Face,
when everywhere
that is all we see?
You are
as You praise
Your-Self—
Eternal
Source of All Being,
Satisfier of All Needs,
we die in You
and are resurrected
in Truth,
that the tablets
of these hearts

---

23 *Kun, fa Yakun:* "Be" – and it is. An expression of the immediacy and infinitude of God's Will, this phrase appears numerous times in the Quran, as in verse 36:82, page 106.

might shine
in Your Light,
that we might witness
all the songs of Your Love
that You keep chanting,
Ya Samad,
Ya Baqi,
Ya Haqq,
Ya Hafiz, Ya Wadud.

Ya Hafiz, O Preserver, *Ya Hadi*, O Guide,
Ya Hamid, O Most Praised and Praiseworthy,
Ya Samad, O Eternal, Satisfier of All Needs,
Ya Baqi, O Abiding One, *Ya Haqq*, O Truth,
Ya Wadud, O Love

*But all the while God encompasses them
without their being aware of it.
Nay, but this is a discourse sublime,
inscribed upon an imperishable tablet.*
[85: 20–22]

*Behold, it is We Ourselves who have bestowed from on high,
step by step, this reminder:
and, behold, it is We who shall truly guard it.*
[15:9]

*Muhammad is the Messenger of God;
and those who are with him stand firm
when facing those who deny the Truth,
and are compassionate with each other.
You can see them bow and prostrate themselves in prayer,
seeking grace from God and His good pleasure.
On their faces are their marks, traced by prostration.*

This is their parable in the Torah,
and their parable in the Gospel:
like a seed which sends forth its shoot, which grows strong,
so that it becomes thick, and then stands firm on its stem,
delighting those who sow with wonder.
[48:29]

Consider the sky and the night-visitor.
And what will explain to you what the night-visitor is?
It is the star of piercing brightness.
There is no soul that does not have a protector over it.
[86:1–4]

And when Moses came to Our appointed place,
and his Sustainer spoke to him, he said:
"O my Sustainer! Show me, that I might behold You!"
He said: "Never can you see Me, but look at this mountain:
if it remains in its place, then—only then— will you see Me."
And as soon as his Sustainer revealed His/Her glory to the mountain,
He/She made it crumble to dust, and Moses fell down in a swoon.
And when he came to himself,
he said: "Limitless are You in Your glory!
Unto You do I turn, and I am of the original in faith!"
He said: "O Moses! Behold,
I have purified you for the sake of the people
with My Messages and with My Words.
So hold fast unto what I have entrusted to you,
and be among those who give thanks!"
[7:143–144]

I call to witness the coming-down in portions—
and, behold, this is indeed a mighty affirmation, if you but knew it!
Witness, this is a truly noble discourse, in a Book well-guarded,
which none but the pure of heart shall touch:
a revelation from the Sustainer of all the worlds!
[56:75–80]

Thus has God, the Almighty, the Wise, revealed to you,
and unto those who preceded you:
His / Hers is all that is in the heavens and all that is on earth;
and Most Exalted, Magnificent is She / He.
The uppermost heavens are well-nigh rent asunder in awe;
and the angels extol their Sustainer's limitless glory and praise,
and ask forgiveness for all who are on earth.
Oh, truly, God alone is Oft Forgiving, Infinitely Compassionate!
And as for those who take anything
beside Him / Her for their protectors—
God watches over and preserves them,
and for their conduct you are not responsible.
[42:3–6]

But, truly, your Sustainer—He / She alone—
is Almighty, Infinitely Compassionate!
Now, behold, this has indeed been bestowed
from on high by the Sustainer of all the worlds:
trustworthy divine inspiration
has alighted with it from on high upon your heart.
[26:191–194]

Wherever you turn, there is the Face of God.
[2:115]

For He / She is the Creator Supreme in skill and knowledge!
Truly, when He / She intends a thing,
His / Her command is "Be"—and it is.
So glory to Him / Her in whose hands is the dominion over all things;
and to Him / Her will you all return.
[36:81–83]

39. Al Muqit, The Nourisher

Ya Muqit, Ya Razzaq, Ya Quddus, Ya Qadir, Ya Wadud, Ya Wasi

O You who nourish us,
O You who provide for all our needs,
who heal us when we are ill,
realign our voices
that they might resonate
with Your Most Holy vibrations.
It is Your Power
through which we speak,
or think,
or sing songs in praise
of Your Vast Presence
that inundates
and irradiates every thing that is,
within the compass of our sight,
our hearing, our knowing,
and all that is hidden
from these limited senses,
until You open the doors
of Your perception
through these capacities
that You have given,
and we begin to see
Your dancing radiance
through which You feed our hearts,
the birds, the animals, the stars.
You keep pouring sustenance
down throats of every part of us.
And when something is out
of balance,
it is You who restores it
and heals from within

the cells that keep rejuvenating
through Your Love—
how else could we walk
upon this earth,
could we dance through this air,
and swim in Your seas,
with our brother and sister whales
who leap with joy
at the sound of Your Name
chanted through the beating
of their hearts?
"I see the Sea where I can swim,"
says Shams, "come, join me there."[24]
There is no end to Your water,
through which you nourish us—
through every part of us,
singing songs of our existence,
even through our hair,
and rectifying our intentions,
our memories,
through past generations
and forward through children
who have yet to be born.
O Gracious Sustainer,
purify these hearts
and let us know Your Love
in all its Vastness,
before and behind us,
above and below,
to the right and the left,
and within every fiber of our being,
until Your Compassion and Mercy

---

[24] Words of Shams of Tabriz: Excerpt from *Rumi's Sun, the Teachings of Shams of Tabriz*, the mentor and beloved spiritual friend of Jalaluddin Rumi, p.13.

pour out of us,
and Your Beauty,
Truth is seen.

Ya Muqit, O Nourisher, *Ya Razzaq*, O Provider of All,
Ya Quddus, O Most Holy and Pure,
Ya Qadir, O Apportioner of Power,
Ya Wasi, O All Encompassing Vastness,
Ya Khabir, O All Aware,
Ya Sami, O All Hearing, *Ya Basir*, O All Seeing,
Ya Nur, O You Who Are Light, *Ya 'Alim*, O All Knowing,
Ya Rahman, O Infinitely Compassionate One,
Ya Rahim, O Infinitely Merciful,
Ya Haqq, O Truth, *Ya Jamil*, O Beauty,
Ya Wadud, O Love

How many are the creatures that do not carry their own sustenance!
It is God who feeds them and you:
for He/She is the One Who Hears, The One Who Knows.
[29:60]

The Infinitely Compassionate!
It is He/She Who has taught the Quran.
He/She has created the human being.
He/She has taught them clear thought and speech.
The sun and the moon follow their designated paths;
and the herbs and the trees—both bow in adoration.
And He/She has raised high the heavens,
and He/She has devised a balance
so that you might not measure wrongly.
So weigh justly and don't measure lightly.
And the earth He/She has outspread for all creatures
with fruit on it and date-palms bearing enclosed clusters

and grain on tall stalks and sweetly fragrant plants;
which then of your Sustainer's blessings will you deny?
[55:1–13]

To Him/Her belong the keys of the heavens and the earth;
He/She grants abundant sustenance
or bestows it in meager measure to whom He/She wills:
for He/She knows well all things.
[42:12]

Say: "That which is from the Presence of God is better
than any bargain or passing delight!
For God is the Best of Providers."
[62:11]

And if all the trees on earth were pens and the Ocean were ink
with seven Oceans behind it to add to it
still, the Words of God would not be exhausted:
for God is Exalted in Power, All Wise.
[31:27]

"Every human being is a word of God. What word are you?"
[~ Shams of Tabriz, *Rumi's Sun, the Teachings of Shams of Tabriz*]

O children of Adam!
Indeed, We have given you garments to cover your nakedness,
and as a thing of beauty;
but the garment of God-consciousness is best of all.
This is one of God's messages—
that human beings might take it to heart.
[7:26]

40. Al Hasib, The Reckoner

Ya Hasib

One year ending,
another opening—
You give us moments
to take account
of all the passages
of our lives—
Ya Hasib,
You who know
the good and the harm,
and the secrets
of all hearts.
You recognize
when we are fed,
and when we are hungry
for love,
and how our actions
compensate
for what we feel
we lack,
and yet,
You are always here,
with Your rectifying balance,
Ya Muqsit,
You who pour munificence
from the eternal
point of Sustenance
deep within these hearts;
invisible streams
of Grace arrive
through the vortex
of Your Love.

What is this magnetism
that lets us know
if we are true
or false?
An inner Compass,
a taste,
that enables us
to reckon
each day,
each moment,
not waiting
for some distant
resurrection,
but recognizing
now
the possibility
of awakening—
and keep your connection
that you may find
felicity.
Gratitude quakes through us
for all the ways
You gift us,
with knowing
rectitude,
and capacities
for standing
straight
and bowing
humbly
before Your Face
that everywhere
is seeing us
and allowing
us to witness
that Infinite Generosity

of Your
All Comprehending
Presence,
Ya Wasi, Ya Karim,
Ya Basir, Ya Hasib,
Ya Muqsit, Ya Shahid,
Ya 'Alim, Ya Shakur,
Ya Mumin,
Ya Mu'id, Ya Wadud.
O You who refresh and restore everything
with Your Overwhelming Love.

Ya Hasib, O Reckoner,
Ya Wasi, O All Encompassing One,
Ya Karim, O Infinitely Generous One,
Ya Basir, O All Seeing One,
Ya Muqsit, O Keeper of the Balance,
Ya Shahid, O Witness, *Ya 'Alim*, O All Knowing One,
Ya Shakur, O Grateful One, Ever Responsive to Gratitude,
Ya Mumin, O Most Faithful One,
Ya Mu'id, O Restorer, *Ya Wadud*, O Infinitely Loving One

To God belongs all that is in the heavens and all that is on earth.
And whether you bring into the open what is in your minds or conceal it,
God will call you to account for it.
[2:284]

And God is sufficient as Reckoner.
[4:6]

With that which God has bestowed on you
seek the Home of the Hereafter,
yet do not forget your portion in this world—

do good as God has been good to you
and do not seek to do harm in the land.
[28:77]

God watches over everything.
When you are greeted with a greeting of peace,
answer with an even better greeting, or at least with its like.
Truly, God keeps account of all things.
[4:85–86]

Wherever you turn, there is the Face of God.
[2:115]

And keep your connection, and remain conscious of God,
so that you might attain felicity.
[3:200]

In the Name of God the Infinitely Compassionate and Most Merciful:
When the earth shakes with her final convulsion,
and the earth yields up her burdens,
and the human being cries out: "What is the matter with her?"—
on that Day she will declare her tidings:
your Sustainer will have inspired her.
On that Day all human beings will come forward separately
to be shown their deeds.
Then shall anyone who has done an atom's weight of good see it!
And anyone who has done an atom's weight of harm shall see that.
[99:1–8]

"O our Sustainer! Behold, we heard a voice calling to faith:
'Have faith in your Sustainer!' —and so we came to have faith.
O our Sustainer! Forgive us, then, our sins, and erase our ill deeds;
and return us to You with the gently righteous and just!
O our Sustainer, grant us that which You have promised us
through Your messengers,
and do not let us be disgraced on the Day of Standing Straight!

Truly, You never fail to fulfill Your promise!"
And thus does their Sustainer respond to their prayer:
"I shall not let the labors of any of you be lost,
whether man or woman: each of you is a part of the other.
And so, as for those who left behind or were driven from their homes,
who suffer hurt in My Way, and struggle, as though unto death—
I shall most certainly clear from them their ill deeds,
and shall surely bring them into gardens
through which running waters flow,
as recompense from the Presence of God—
for from the Presence of God
is the most beautiful of recompense."
[3:193–195]

41. Al Jalil, The Mightily Majestic One

Ya Jalil, Ya Jamil, Ya Wadud

O You of Infinite Might
and Courage,
instilling our hearts
with the force
to stand for Truth,
the rivers of Your Strength
flow through us
with even greater power
when we recognize
their Source—
from water
everything comes forth;
we move with Your Will.
Hydrogen and Oxygen
combine
and their flammability
becomes fluidity
aligned,
nourishing
plants,
animals,
humans,
clearing the atmosphere
with Your Intention,
Ya Jalil,
creating Beauty
through Your Generosity
flowing
through all that is.
All these sparkles
of Your Creation

will subside
in the stream
of Your Bestowal,
yet forever will abide
Your Face,
Your Love.
Ya Jalil,
Ya Jamil,
Ya Wadud.

> *Ya Jalil*, O Mightily Majestic One,
> *Ya Jamil*, O Most Beautiful One,
> *Ya Wadud*, O Infinitely Loving One

> *And God sends down rain from the skies*
> *and with it bestows life to the earth that was dead:*
> *truly, in this is a sign for those who pay attention.*
> [16:65]

> *We made out of water every living thing.*
> [21:30]

> *And it is God who has created all animals out of water;*
> *and among them are such as crawl on their bellies,*
> *and such as walk on two legs, and such as walk on four.*
> *God creates what He/She wills:*
> *for, truly, God has the power to will anything.*
> *Indeed, from on high have We bestowed messages*
> *clearly showing the truth;*
> *but God guides onto a straight way*
> *he or she who wills [to be guided].*
> [24:45–46]

*Among the desert dwellers, there are those who have faith in Allah,
and the Day of Return,
and consider what he or she spends as a means
of drawing them nearer to God
and blessings of the Messengers.
Truly, it is a means of nearness for them.
God will admit them to His/Her Mercy;
Truly, God is Oft Forgiving, Infinitely Merciful.*
[9:99]

Truly, God loves those who are conscious of Him/Her.
[9:7]

*All that lives on earth or in the heavens
is bound to pass away, but forever will abide
Your Sustainer's Face, full of Majesty and Glory.*
[55:26–27]

42. Al Karim, The Infinitely Generous One

Ya Karim, Ya Wahhab, Ya Wadud

"Dealings with the Generous
are not difficult."[25]
May we be of those—
who offer words of compassion
and funds from the pockets
with which You have gifted us,
not with any agenda,
but solely *seeking Your Face* . . .
for It is here,
everywhere among us—
Jesus also told us:
"And to the least . . ."
If we choose to give,
You *ease our Way*
to Bliss,
the felicity of being
in the flowing of Your Love.
If the Seas were ink,
never would Your Love's expression
be exhausted.
We lend our ears,
our hearts and our hands

---

25 ~ Mevlana Jalaluddin Rumi [*Mathnawi:* Book I: 218–221]:

> Love of the living is every moment fresher than a bud
> in the spirit and in the sight.
> Choose the love of that Living One who is everlasting,
> who gives you to drink of the wine that increases life.
> Choose the love of Him from whose love
> all the prophets gained power and glory.
> Do not say, "We have no admission to that King."
> Dealings with the generous are not difficult.

to serve
Your calling.
All that is in heaven
and on earth
shares stories of Your Glory,
for Truly,
You are limitless in Your Bounty
and Your Graciousness,
every moment
extending Your Hand
through ours.
Ya Karim,
Ya Wahhab,
Ya Wadud.

Ya Karim, O Most Generous,
Ya Wahhab, O Overwhelmingly Generous One,
Ya Wadud, O Love

So, the one who gives to others and stands in awe of God,
and sincerely affirms that which is Best—
We will indeed ease for him/her the path to bliss . . .
the one who is truly conscious of God:
the one who spends his/her possessions upon others
so that he or she might grow in purity—
not as payment for favors received,
but only out of a longing for the Countenance of his/her Sustainer,
the All Highest:
and such, indeed, shall in time be well-pleased.
[92:5–7; 92:18–21]

Truly, my Sustainer is the One Who Is Truly Rich,
Most Generous!
[27:40]

"For I was hungry, and ye gave me meat:
I was thirsty, and ye gave me drink:
I was a stranger, and ye took me in:
naked, and ye clothed me:
I was sick, and ye visited me:
I was in prison, and ye came unto me."
Then shall the righteous answer him, saying,
"Lord, when saw we thee hungry, and fed thee?
or thirsty, and gave thee drink?
When saw we thee a stranger, and took thee in?
or naked, and clothed thee?
Or when saw we thee sick, or in prison, and came unto thee?"
And the King shall answer and say unto them,
"Truly I say unto you,
Inasmuch as ye have done it
unto one of the least of these my brethren,
ye have done it unto me."
[The Bible, Matthew, 25:35–45]

Truly, as for those who attain to faith and do righteous deeds—
the gardens of paradise will be there to welcome them;
therein will they abide; nor will they desire any change therefrom.
Say: "If all the sea were ink for my Sustainer's words,
the sea would indeed be exhausted
before my Sustainer's words are exhausted!
And even if We were to add to it sea upon sea."
Say: "I am but a mortal man like all of you;
the inspiration has come to me that your God is God, the One.
So whoever looks forward to meeting his/her Sustainer,
let him/her do deeds of wholeness and reconciliation."
[18:107–110]

In the Name of God, the Infinitely Compassionate and Infinitely Merciful:
All that is in the heavens and all that is on earth
extols the limitless glory of God,
the Supreme Sovereign, the Holy, the Almighty, the All Wise!
He/She it is who has sent unto the unlettered people

a messenger from among themselves,
to convey unto them His/Her Signs, and to cause them to grow in purity,
and to impart to them revelation as well as wisdom—
whereas before that they were, indeed, clearly in error—
and from them unto others who have not yet joined them:
for He/She is Almighty, All Wise!
Such is God's Bounty: He/She grants it to anyone who is willing:
for God is limitless in His/Her Great Bounty.
[62:1–4]

The Hand of God is over their hands.
[48:10]

43. Ar Raqib, The Ever Watchful One

Ya Raqib, Ya Mujib, Ya Karim

Dawn—
a single cardinal
calling "Raqib"—
the Watcher
is always here—
holding us
with the Endless Generosity
of Al Karim,
and the Continual Response to Prayer
of Al Mujib.
Red in the sunrise,
warm in color
and in heart—
the Watcher is
caring for creation,
always attending
to our need,
Witness, Ash Shahid,
to all the unfoldings
of our lives,
and to Your own Magnificence
permeating every cell
and atom of existence.
Ya Raqib—
there is one within us, too,
You
Who Watch Over Our Hearts
and the function
of each organ
and how it does its part
to keep us moving

in the stream of Love,
flowing into Your Sea
where, as candles
set upon leaves,
we float
into Your Infinity,
an offering of beauty
You will never forget,
for You are the Watcher,
the One Who Responds to Our Prayer,
the Most Subtly and Overwhelmingly Generous,
Ya Karim, Ya Mujib, Ya Raqib.

Ya Raqib, O Ever Watchful One,
Ash Shahid, The Witness,
Ya Mujib, O You Who Respond to Prayer,
Ya Karim, O Most Generous One

And God keeps watch over everything.
[33:52]

*Don't they observe the birds above them
spreading their wings and folding them in?
None can uphold them except the Most Gracious:
truly, it is He/She Who watches over all things.*
[67:19]

*O humankind, be conscious of Your Sustainer,
who created you from a single soul,
and created out of it, its mate,
and out of the two spread out countless men and women;
reverence God, in whose name you ask your mutual rights,
and reverence the wombs that bore you;
for, truly, God ever watches over you.*
[4:1]

And He/She alone holds sway over His/Her servants.
And He/She sends forth heavenly forces to watch over you.
[6:61]

It was We who created the human being
and We know what his inmost self whispers within him,
for We are nearer to him than his jugular vein.
Whenever the two demands of his nature come face to face,
contending from the right and the left,
not a word does he utter but there is a watcher with him, ever-present.
And the dazzlement of death will bring truth before his eyes.
[50:16–19]

And if My servants ask you about Me—witness, I am near;
I respond to the call of the one who calls,
whenever he/she calls Me:
let them, then, respond to Me, and have faith in Me,
so that they may follow the right way.
[2:186]

44. Al Mujib, The One Who Responds

Ya Mujib, Ya Raqib, Ya Wadud

Ya Mujib,
You who make us happy
in Your Graciousness,
You hear and answer,
even when we stumble in our asking.
You know best
how to respond,
for You are watching, Ya Raqib.
What would we do without Your clouds?
How would the rains come,
how would our gardens freshen
and flourish?
Darkness brings new life.
How could we continue,
if we had no rest?
Families sustain us
and require our care.
There is really very little
that we need.
Whales dove back into the sea
and left behind possessions.
Now they sing deep songs
and breathe, every breath,
consciously.
Their family ties remain;
and mothers traverse a six month fast
to birth and nurse their young.
What food do we ask of You?
What relations do we seek?
Is the greenness shining in our eyes,
reflecting from Your Gifts?

Does honey fall from our lips?
"Call upon Me;
I will answer,"
You have said.
We vouchsafed revelation unto Moses,
and appointed his brother Aaron
to help him to bear his burden.
Brothers,
sisters, all,
we are called,
to respond to those in need.
And in this service,
we are freed,
from the bondage of desire
that might
drag us to the depths of the pits,
from which only Your Hand
might save us.
Joseph knew reliance
on Your Word
and held the rope
of trust in Your Love;
You raised him to the highest station.
Visions inundated
and buoyed his heart
through the time of drought.
Your remembrance lights
our way.
Our call is Your call to us,
and together we sing songs
of the Ocean of Your Love.

Ya Mujib, O You Who Respond,
Ya Raqib, O You Who Are Ever Watchful,
Ya Wadud, O Infinitely Loving One

Call upon Me; I will answer.
[40:60]

And, indeed, We vouchsafed revelation unto Moses,
and appointed his brother Aaron to help him to bear his burden.
[25:35]

Indeed, in [the story of] Joseph and his brothers
there are messages for all who seek . . . .
We gave unto Joseph a firm place on earth;
and so that We might impart unto him
some understanding of the inner meaning of happenings.
For God always prevails in whatever is His/Her purpose:
but most people know it not.
And when he reached full manhood,
We bestowed upon him the ability to discern,
as well as inner knowing:
for thus do We reward the doers of good.
[12:7; 12:21–22]

"I desire no more than to set things to rights
in so far as it lies within my power;
but the achievement of my aim depends on God alone.
In Him/Her have I placed my trust,
and to Him/Her do I always turn!"
[11:88, saying of the Prophet Shuʻayb]

True piety does not consist in turning your faces
towards the east or the west—
but truly pious is he or she who has faith in God,
and the Day of Return, and the angels,
and revelation, and the prophets;
and spends his or her substance—
however much he or she may cherish it—
upon the near of kin, and the orphans,
and the needy, and the wayfarer, and the beggars,

and for the freeing of human beings from bondage;
and is constant in prayer, and renders the purifying dues;
and they who keep their promises whenever they promise,
and are patient in misfortune and hardship and in time of peril:
it is they that have proved themselves true,
and it is they, they who are conscious of God.
[2:177]

And unto the Thamud We sent their brother Salih.
He said: "O my people! Worship God:
you have no deity other than Him/Her.
He/She brought you into being from the earth,
and made you thrive upon it.
Ask Him/Her, therefore, to forgive you your mistakes,
and then turn towards Him/Her in repentance—
for, truly, my Sustainer is Ever Near, Ever Responsive to your call!"
[11:61]

Yes! You were praying to your Sustainer for help,
and then He/She responded to you:
"Truly, I shall aid you with a thousand angels
following one after another!"
And God conferred this solely as a glad tiding,
that by it your hearts should be set at rest—
since no help can come from any but God:
truly, God is Almighty, Most Wise!
Remember how it was when He/She caused inner calm to enfold you,
as an assurance from Him/Her,
and sent down over you water from the skies
so that by it He/She might purify you
and free you from the unclean whisperings of Satan
and strengthen your hearts and so make your steps firm.
Witness! Your Sustainer inspired the angels
to convey His/Her message to the faithful:
"I am with you!"
[8:9–12]

45. Al Wasi, The Infinite, All Encompassing

Ya Wasi, Ya Wadud, Ya 'Alim

O You Who Are Infinite,
All Encompassing,
Your Heavens open
and we fall through—
up,
into such vast expanses
we lose our bearings
and relinquish
all we are carrying
of injustices
and justices waiting
to be balanced
by Your Will.
We rest
in the upward draft
of Your breezes
bringing us near.
Wouldn't we want
to let go of any ballast
holding us back?
Earth is beautiful
but complex
in its relationship of elements;
let go into the air,
and freer still,
the ether,
beyond even the stars
that hold their places
through Your Command.
In one breath
we can traverse the galaxies.

There is no ceiling
to our knowing;
the way is open.
You have made us
in Your Image,
some would say—
in this inner vastness
our hearts and minds encompass,
though our frames be small.
And yet the very atoms
of our structure
disappear from sight
when scientists attempt
to measure
the range of our function.
Infinite universes within,
infinite universes without,
through the looking-glass
of You
we see stars
twinkling everywhere
as this semblance of self
disappears
within the fineness
of Your air breathing us,
Your breath being us,
just beside You,
in and out,
until this Vastness
is all there is.
La illaha il Allah!
Ya Wasi, Ya Wadud,
Ya 'Alim.

Ya Wasi, O You Who Are Infinite, All Encompassing,
Ya Wadud, O Most Loving One,

Ya 'Alim, O Knower of All,
La illaha il Allah, There is no reality but the Reality,
nothing truly exists but Divinity

Say: "Behold, all bounty is in the Hand of God;
He/She grants it unto whom He/She wills:
for God is Infinite, All Encompassing, All Knowing.
[3:73]

Now await in patience the command of your Sustainer:
for truly you are within Our sight.
And celebrate the praises of your Sustainer
whenever you arise,
and for part of the night also praise Him/Her
and at the retreat of the stars!
[52:48–49]

God—there is no deity but Hu,
the Ever Living, the Self-Subsisting Source of all Being.
No slumber can seize Him/Her nor sleep.
All things in heaven and on earth belong to Hu.
Who could intercede in His/Her Presence
without His/Her permission?
He/She knows what appears in front of
and behind His/Her creatures.
Nor can they encompass any knowledge of Him/Her
except what He/She wills.
His/Her throne extends over the heavens and the earth,
and He/She feels no fatigue in guarding and preserving them,
for He/She is the Highest and Most Exalted.
[2:255]

We will show them Our signs on the farthest horizons
and within their own selves
until the Truth becomes clear to them.

Is it not enough that your Sustainer is Witness to all things?
Indeed! Are they in doubt concerning the Meeting with their Sustainer?
Ah, truly! it is He/She Who encompasses all things!
[41:53–54]

46. Al Hakim, The Truly Wise, Healer of All Our Ills

Ya Hakim, Al 'Adl, Ya Wadud

Ya Hakim,
O Most Wise Healer of Hearts,
You judge between us when our intentions go awry;
You help us to rebalance,
to begin again
with Your Knowing
and Your Love.
The dawn arrives
with a breeze of refreshment
carrying Your dew to our lips,
that we might drink of Your Wisdom
that has come for us in the night,
and begin again.
Those who are patient in adversity,
and true to their word,
and truly devout, and who spend in God's way,
and pray for forgiveness from their innermost hearts before dawn.
God offers signs—and so do the angels
and all who are endowed with knowledge—
that there is no god except God, the Upholder of Justice:
there is no deity but Hu,
the Almighty, the Truly Wise.
Ya Hakim,
Ya Wadud.

Ya Hakim, O You Who Are Truly Wise,
Healer of All Our Ills,
Al 'Adl, The Most Just,
Ya Wadud, O Infinitely Loving One

O you who have attained to faith!
If you remain conscious of God,
He/She will endow you with a standard by which to discern
the true from the false,
and will clear evil from you,
and will forgive you your mistakes:
for God is limitless in the abundance of His/Her blessing.
[8:29]

The bestowal of this Book pours down from God,
the Almighty, the Truly Wise.
We have not created the heavens and the earth
and all that is between them
except in accordance with an inner truth,
and for a determined term.
[46:2–3]

For unto Him/Her belongs every being
that is in the heavens and on earth;
all things devoutly obey His/Her will.
And He/She it is who creates all in the beginning,
and then brings it forth anew: and most easy is this for Him/Her,
since His/Hers is the essence of all that is most sublime
in the heavens and on earth,
and He/She alone is Most Mighty, Wisest of the Wise.
[30:26–27]

Remain conscious of God,
O you who are endowed with insight—
who have attained to faith!
God has indeed bestowed on you a reminder from on high:
through a messenger who conveys to you God's clear messages,
so that He/She might lead
those who have attained to faith and do rightful deeds
out of the depths of darkness into the light.
And whoever has faith in God and does what is right and just,

He/She will admit them into gardens through which running waters flow,
there to abide beyond the count of time:
indeed, a most goodly provision will God have granted him/her!
[65:10–11]

Those who are patient in adversity, and true to their word,
and truly devout, and who spend in God's way,
and pray for forgiveness from their innermost hearts before dawn.
God offers signs—and so do the angels
and all who are endowed with knowledge—
that there is no god except God, the Upholder of Justice:
there is no deity but Hu, the Almighty, the Truly Wise.
Witness—the only true religion in the sight of God
is self-surrender to Him/Her.
[3:17–19]

47. Al Wadud, The Infinitely Loving

Ya Wadud, Ya Wali, Ya Wakil

O Love,
continually,
You are watching
out for us,
holding our hand
when we are ill,
soothing our brow
when we are troubled,
bringing Peace
to our hearts
when we have struggled
in Your Way
and come
to know Your Presence
with us,
in love with us
so much,
that we have recognized
the Love in us
that seeds our being
and makes the clouds weep
to clear these hearts
and skies of Your heavens.
As with Solomon's dove
beside the stair,
You are calling us;
and when we call,
You answer.
You have promised.
Our Beloved is here—
You are our Friend,

our Protector,
the Guardian of All Our Affairs,
the One
who sings
the songs of Resurrection,
restoring all to its deepest Beauty
in the Garden
of Your Eternal
and Everlasting
Love.
Ya Ahad,
Ya Ba'ith,
Ya Mu'id,
Ya Nur al Quddus,
Ya Baqi,
Ya Wali,
Ya Wakil,
Ya Wadud!

Ya Wadud, O Infinite Love,
Ya Wali, O Friend and Protector,
Ya Wakil, O Guardian of All Our Affairs,
Ya Ahad, O You Who Are One,
Ya Ba'ith, O You Who Resurrect,
Ya Mu'id, O You Who Restore,
Ya Nur al Quddus, O Light of the Most Holy and Pure,
Ya Baqi, O Everlasting, Abiding One

He/She loves them and they love Him/Her.
[5: 54]

Witness, Your Sustainer inspired the angels
to convey His/Her message to the faithful:
I am with you.
[8:12]

Call upon Me; I will answer.
[40:60]

Ask your Sustainer for forgiveness, and turn to Him/Her:
for truly, my Sustainer is Infinitely Merciful and Infinitely Loving.
[11:90]

And paradise will be brought near to the God-conscious,
no longer will it be distant: "This is what was promised for you—
to everyone who would turn to God
and keep Him/Her always in remembrance—
who stood in awe of the Most Compassionate though unseen
and brought a heart turned in devotion to Him/Her.
Enter here in peace and security; this is the Day of eternal Life!"
There will be for them there all that they may wish
and yet more in Our Presence.
[50:31–35]

God has promised the faithful, both men and women,
gardens beneath which running waters flow,
there to abide
and fair dwellings in gardens of enduring bliss;
but God's good acceptance is the greatest bliss of all—
for this is the ultimate success!
[9:72]

And in heaven is your sustenance and all that which you are promised.
Then by the Sustainer of heaven and earth, this is the Truth—
as true as the fact that you are able to speak.
[51:23]

O my dove, that art in the clefts of the rock,
in the secret places of the stairs,
let me see thy countenance, let me hear thy voice;
for sweet is thy voice, and thy countenance is comely.
[The Bible, Song of Solomon, 2:14]

He brought me to the banquet house
and his banner over me was Love.
[The Bible, Song of Solomon, 2:4]

Truly, those who have faith and do rightful deeds
of wholeness and reconciliation,
the Most Gracious will endow with Love.
[19:96]

48. Al Majeed, The Sublimely Majestic

Ya Majeed, Ya Fattah, Ya Wadud, Ya Rahim

Ya Majeed,
every day You paint
the sky with glory,
and even with the autumn paling,
You descend the leaves
in armfuls of red and gold!
How could we not know
the Glory of Your Face,
Your signature upon our hearts,
Your writing on the hills,
when they bask in Your sun
and reveal the shadows of the clouds
in songs of light
echoing to our hearts
with the affirmation of the birds,
who glorify You every morning?
In sound and light
all of nature sings Your praises,
Ya Majeed,
and *the stars and trees*
bow down in love with You,
who have created all this panoply
of grace abounding
and draw the waters
up
even from the hardest rock,
that splits before Your Willing
of Generosity
and Kindness,
Ya Karim,
Ya Rauf.

May we learn
to allow
the hard shells to crack open,
and to know
that even in that pain
there is Mercy,
Great Mercy emerging through it,
with the pure water
that restores and nourishes,
for Your Glory is only ever manifested
from the root of Love,
*For I have willed upon Myself
the law of Compassion and Mercy,*
and *My Mercy overwhelms everything!*
Ya Majeed, Ya Fattah,
Ya Wadud, Ya Rahim.

Ya Majeed, O Sublimely Majestic One,
Ya Fattah, O You Who Open the Way,
Ya Wadud, O Infinitely Loving One,
Ya Rahim, O Infinitely Merciful,
Ya Rahman, O Infinitely Compassionate,
Ya Karim, O Most Generous, *Ya Rauf*, O Most Kind

Before Him/Her prostrate the stars and the trees.
[55:6]

*And when his people asked Moses for water,
We inspired him, "Strike the rock with your staff!"—
then twelve springs gushed forth from it,
so that all the people knew where to drink.
And We caused the clouds to comfort them with their shade,
and We sent down to them manna and quails,
"Partake of the good things
which We have provided for you as sustenance."*
[7:160]

*Your Sustainer has willed upon Himself/Herself
the law of Compassion and Mercy.*
[6: 54]

*"The grace of God and His/Her blessings be upon you,
O people of this House!
Truly, Ever Worthy of Praise, Sublimely Majestic is She/He!"*
[11:73]

*"Truly, I have come to love the love of all that is good
because I bear my Sustainer in mind!"*
[38:32, words of the Prophet Solomon]

My Mercy overwhelms everything.
[7:156]

49. Al Ba'ith, The Resurrector

Ya Ba'ith, Ya Baqi

O You who Resurrect us
with Peace
after the turbulence
of storms,
when we have
lost our bearings
and despaired
of finding Home,
perhaps even
lost our lives
in distant lands,
You find us,
and welcome us
back
to stand
up among Your blessed friends
near the Throne
of Almightiness
by Your Command
that electrifies
our lifeless bones,
and hearts
begin to sing again
with the Joy
of knowing You.
Water returns
to parched throats
and moisture
to this skin
and all manner
of fruits are here

for us
in the Garden
of Your Love,
O Abiding One.
The tangles
of our days and nights
are eased,
and everywhere
we meet each other,
we smile
and pass from hand
to hand
and heart to heart
the knowledge
of Your Love
and pearls of Peace.
Ya Wadud,
Ya Salaam,
Ya Wajid,
Ya Quddus.

Ya Ba'ith, O Resurrector,
Ya Baqi, O Abiding Everlasting One,
Ya Wadud, O Infinitely Loving One,
Ya Salaam, O You Who Are Peace,
Ya Wajid, O You Who Find Us and Bring Us Home,
Ya Quddus, O Holy, Most Pure

Truly, your Sustainer's grasp is strong.
It is He/She who creates from the very beginning
and it is He/She who can restore.
And He/She is Ever Ready to Forgive, the Loving One,
Lord of the Throne of Glory,
the Unceasing Doer of all that He/She intends.
[85:12–16]

*And call to Him / Her with awe and longing:
truly, God's grace is very near those who do good.
And He / She it is who sends the winds
as joyous news of His / Her coming grace—
so that, when they have brought heavy clouds
We may drive them towards dead land and cause rain to descend;
that by it We may cause all manner of fruitfulness to spring forth.
Even so shall We cause the dead to emerge—
perhaps you will remember.*
[7:56–57]

*And with them companions pure, most beautiful of eye,
like pearls hidden in their shells,
a reward for what they did—
no empty talk will they hear there, nor any call to sin,
but only the tiding of inner soundness and peace.
As for those who have attained to righteousness—
what of those who have attained to righteousness:
amid fruitful lote-trees,
and flowering acacias, and sheltering shade, and waters gushing,
and abundant fruit, never-failing and never out of reach.*
[56:22–33]

The Hand of God is over their hands.
[48:10]

*Truly the companions of the Garden
shall that Day be wholly immersed in joy;
they and their companions will rest on couches in shady groves;
fruits will be there for them,
and theirs shall be whatever they could ask for;
"Peace!"—the Word of a Most Merciful Sustainer!*
[36:55–58]

50. Ash Shahid, The Witness

Ash Shahid, Al Quddus, Ya Karim

Ash Shahid, Al Quddus,
You witness with us
the purity of our intention
and the outcome of all that unfolds.
Your trees burn bright with Your blessing,
guiding us
Home.
With clear eyes,
Truth emerges,
and hearts attuned
hear Your whispers in the night.
Day returns
in Revelation,
a seeing
we can only simulate
if we are listening—
broad bands
of windows
across our house
will let Your music in.
You tell the Truth;
we are learning
in this School of Love
to bear the Truth,
even when it weighs heavy
on our hearts.
You wring us out,
for the honey
they might drip—
to heal a wound,
or light a candle

with the waxen chambers
we've constructed,
melting in Your Presence.
Cell by cell
we witness and release,
like the bees;
You would have us know
what records we've been keeping
that we might rectify
and testify to You,
there is no god but God,
and kneel our egos down
in remembrance,
breath by breath,
as Your elevator
brings us up
into the Rose Garden
of Your Mercy,
Ya Shahid,
Ya Karim,
Ya Rahim,
Ya Haqq.

Ya Shahid, O Witness, *Al Quddus*, The Most Holy Pure One,
Ya Karim, O You Who Are Infinitely Generous,
Ya Rahim, O Infinitely Merciful One,
Ya Haqq, O Truth

O you who have attained to faith!
Always be steadfast in upholding justice,
bearing witness to the truth for God's sake,
even though it may be against your own selves
or your parents and kinsfolk.
Whether the person concerned be rich or poor,

God's claim takes precedence over the claims of either.
Do not, then, follow your own desires,
that you might not turn aside from that which is just.
For if you distort the truth, witness,
God is indeed well-aware of all that you do!
[4:135]

Witness, the only true religion in the sight of God
is self-surrender to Him/Her.
[3:19]

And your God is the One God:
There is no deity but God,
the Infinitely Compassionate, the Infinitely Merciful.
[2:163]

And your Sustainer inspired the bee
to build its cells in mountains, in trees, and in dwelling places,
then to eat of all that the earth produces,
and to skilfully find the spacious paths of its Lord.
Witness how there issues from within their bodies
a drink of varied hues, containing healing for human beings:
truly, in all this is a sign for those who reflect!
[16:68–69]

Have you ever considered the fire which you kindle?
Is it you who have brought into being the tree
which feeds the fire, or is it We who cause it to grow?
It is We who have made it a reminder
and a comfort for those who wander in the wilderness.
Then celebrate the limitless glory of the Name of your Sustainer,
the Most High.
[56:71–74]

For all those who listen to God and the Messenger
are among those on whom God has bestowed His blessings:

the prophets, and those who never deviated from the truth,
and those who with their lives bore witness to the truth,
and the righteous ones; and what a beautiful friendship this is.
Such is the abundance of God—
and it suffices that God is All Knowing.
[4:69–70]

And God said: "Behold, I shall be with you!
If you are constant in prayer, and spend in charity,
and have faith in My messengers and aid them,
and offer up unto God a goodly loan,
I will surely efface your ill deeds
and bring you into gardens
through which running waters flow.
[5:12]

51. Al Haqq, The Truth

Ya Haqq, Ya Batin, Az Zahir

Newly awakened,
we witness Truth,
resplendent in the sunrise
and every color of the rainbow—
It fits itself into any shape
and walks around
to manifest relationship.
Interwoven, Truth to Truth
we realign our strands
of DNA, magnetized
in strength of You;
we know the Truth
when we see it,
when we hear it,
when we taste it
by heart,
and our soul's thirst
is allayed
in that moment,
as we drink
and again open for another
long sip,
and another . . . .
"The Prophet's thirst
was never quenched."[26]
He kept calling to the Truth,
within each human being,
to emerge into the Light;

---

[26] Rumi's words to Shams of Tabriz in response to his question when they first met.

You keep nourishing us
through each other,
and everything that is—
brilliant upon the horizon
and within our hearts—
nestled close beside You,
within You,
through You,
breath by Breath
poured out into this universe.
Ya Haqq, Ya Batin az Zahir.

Ya Haqq, O You Who Are Truth,
Ya Batin, O You Who Are Intimately Hidden,
Az Zahir, The One Who Is Most Clearly Manifest,
Ya Batin az Zahir, O You Who Are the Hidden of the Manifest

And He/She it is who has created the heavens and the earth
in accordance with an inner Truth.
And the Day He/She says, "Be," it is.
His/Her word is the Truth.
[6:73]

Say: "The Truth is from your Sustainer."
[18:29]

As to those who have faith and work righteousness,
truly, We shall not allow to perish
the recompense of anyone who does a good deed.
[18:30]

So set your face steadily and truly to the faith,
turning away from all that is false
according to the pattern with which He has created humankind;
do not allow to be corrupted that which God has made.

That is the true way.
[30:30]

And say: "O my Sustainer!
Cause me to enter upon whatever I may do in a true and sincere way,
and cause me to complete it in a true and sincere way,
and grant me, out of Your Grace, sustaining strength!"
And say: "Truth has now arrived,
and falsehood has withered away:
for, witness, all falsehood is bound to wither away!"
[17:80–81]

O Humankind!
Worship your Sustainer, who has created you
and those who lived before you,
so that you might remain conscious of the One
who has made the earth a resting-place for you and the sky a canopy,
and has sent water down from the sky
and with it brought forth fruits for your sustenance:
then don't claim that there is any power that could rival God,
when you grasp the Truth.
[2:21–22]

God alone is the Ultimate Truth,
and because He/She alone brings the dead to life,
and because He/She has the power to will anything.
[22:6]

Say: "Truly my Sustainer hurls the Truth—
He/She who has complete knowledge of that which is hidden."
Say: "The Truth has arrived,
and falsehood can create nothing new, nor can it revive."
[34:48–49]

We will show them Our signs on the farthest horizons
and within themselves until they know the Truth.
[41:53]

52. Al Wakil, The Guardian of All Affairs

Ya Wakil, Ya Hafiz

Ya Wakil,
O You Who Are the Guardian
of All Our Affairs,
keep us close
and let us know
You care
for all the aspects
of our being
whether blessed by favored stars
or squared by difficulties—
You hold us
and breathe
Your warm breath
through us
to shield us
from the cold
of loss and error—
You know
what is right
and what is wrong
within our hearts
before our inclinations
move us—
keep us near,
steadfast in our watchfulness
through Ar Raqib,
purify our intentions
through al Quddus,
open our hearts
with the generosity
of Al Karim

and Al Wahhab,
that we might keep giving
of ourselves
and know
You are protecting us
and caring for all our cares,
generation upon generation,
as children arise and sing,
O Warith,
You who are the Best Inheritor
of all these hearts
and hearths within
our homes
as we return
to You, the One,
the Living, the Loving,
Ya Ahad, Ya Hayy
Ya Wadud.

> *Ya Wakil*, O You Who Are the Guardian of All Our Affairs,
> *Ya Hafiz*, O Preserver,
> *Ar Raqib*, The Ever Watchful,
> *Al Quddus*, The Most Holy and Pure,
> *Al Karim*, The Most Generous,
> *Al Wahhab*, The Ever Giving, Overcoming All Obstacles,
> *Al Warith*, The Best Inheritor, Who Inherits All,
> *Ya Ahad*, O You Who Are One,
> *Ya Hayy*, O Ever Living,
> *Ya Wadud*, O Infinitely Loving One

In the Name of God, the Infinitely Compassionate and Most Merciful:
O you who are covered!
Stand in prayer by night but not all the night—half of it or a little less,
or a little more; and recite the Quran, slowly and distinctly.
We shall soon send down to you a weighty word.

Truly, the rising by night is the strongest means of governing the soul
and the most appropriate for Words of prayer.
Truly, by day there is a long chain of duties for you;
but keep in remembrance the Name of your Sustainer
and devote yourself to Him / Her wholeheartedly.
Sustainer of the East and the West, there is no god but Hu:
take Him / Her therefore as the Guardian of your affairs.
[73:1–9]

They have been commanded no more than this:
to worship God, offering Him / Her sincere devotion;
to remain constant in prayer; and to give regular charity that purifies;
and that is the True and Straight Way.
[98:5]

In the Name of God, the Infinitely Compassionate and Infinitely Merciful:
Consider the sky and the night-visitor.
And what will explain to you what the night-visitor is?
It is the star of piercing brightness.
There is no soul that does not have a protector over it.
[86:1–4]

"God is enough for us; and how excellent a Guardian is He / She!"—
and they returned with God's blessings and bounty,
without having been touched by harm:
for they had been striving after God's goodly acceptance—
and God is limitless in His / Her great bounty and grace.
[3:173–174]

53. Al Qawi, The Source of All Power

Al Qawi, Al Matin, Al Khaliq, Al Karim

"Not for Love's sake alone did I create you,
but that kindness and generosity might be seen."
The saints have always
known this
and readily
have served
the least
and most distraught
among us
searching for a hand,
a shoulder
upon which to lean.
For they have known
Your Strength
in every fiber
of their being—
how blood courses
with Your breath,
how hearts beat
with Your Love,
how tongues speak
with Your understanding
and feet move
by Your Will.
You Will us
to will Your Kindness,
and to generate
Love,
not hate,
magnetized
by Your centripetal Force

pulling us
to center
where we live
unhindered,
happy
in the Garden
of Your Giving,
extended
in rivers and streams—
re-greening
the whole
of this Creation,
that deserts
might submerge
in the sands,
as water bubbles up
free,
and new lakes
of loving
widen
to the Sea,
sweet,
no longer bitter,
as we merge
in Your proficiency
of water
shining in the sun,
offering itself
to Heaven,
that, purified,
it might return again
to freshen
a parched throat
of bird or fish
or man
or woman

longing
for Your Love.

> *Al Qawi*, The Source of All Power,
> *Al Matin*, The Enduringly Strong,
> *Al Khaliq*, The Creator,
> *Al Karim*, The Infinitely Generous

"I was a Hidden Treasure, and I so loved to be known,
I created the two worlds, seen and Unseen,
in order that My Treasure of Generosity and Loving-kindness
might be known."
[*Hadith Qudsi*]

For God is He/She who gives sustenance—
the Lord of All Power, Steadfast and Everlastingly Strong.
[51:58]

Are you not aware that it is God who sends down water from the skies,
whereupon the earth becomes green?
Truly, God is Most Subtle in Mystery, All Aware.
Unto Him/Her belongs all that is in the heavens and all that is on earth;
and, truly, God—Hu alone—is Rich Without Need,
the One Worthy of All Praise.
[22:63–64]

And God will most certainly support one who supports His/Her endeavor—
for, truly, God is the Source of All Power, Almighty—
those who, if We firmly establish them
on earth, remain constant in prayer, and give in charity,
and enjoin the doing of what is right and forbid the doing of what is wrong;
but with God rests the final outcome of all events.
[22:40–41]

Whatever is in the heavens and on earth
let it declare the praises and glory of God:
for God alone is Almighty, Truly Wise.
To God belongs the dominion of the heavens and the earth;
it is God Who Gives Life and Bestows Death;
and God has Power over all things.
God is the First and the Last, the Manifest and the Hidden,
and Knows completely all things.
It is God who created the heavens and the earth in six aeons
and is firmly settled on the Throne of Power.
[57:1–4]

Witness: the God-conscious will be amid gardens and springs,
taking joy in that which their Sustainer gives them
because before then they had lived a good life:
they would sleep only a little at night
and from the core of their hearts at dawn they would pray for forgiveness;
and of all that they possessed would grant a rightful share
to the one who asked and the one who was not able.
And on earth are signs for those of inner certainty,
and within yourselves.
Will you not then see?
[51:15–21]

54. Al Matin, The One Who Is Ever Steadfast, Everlastingly Strong

Ya Matin, Ya Badi

Your Joy
is coming to the mountainside,
Ya Matin,
with every sunrise.
The breeze of dawn
kisses the shores
of Your hills,
and every day they display
Your Light,
and generous shadows,
in the folds of their skin
where rivers run
and waterfalls tumble
with Your Grace.
Anchoring our world,
they hold Firm in Your Power,
reaching to heaven
with their pyramidal peaks
peeking through
the veils of clouds
to know You
in intimate sky chambers.
As above,
so below.
Their feet, too,
know Your Presence
as deep veins connect
the core of Your Love's traversal,
O Badi,
Most Skilful Creator!

Nightingales burst into song,
perched
upon the trees that rise
so strongly into the fullness
of Your air.
With iron You fortify us
and strengthen our resolve
to see You
everywhere;
with gold You adorn us,
with Your Light You magnify us,
as we stand with the mountains
in the Glory of Your Dawn,
opening our arms
for Your Embrace,
Ya Wasi,
Ya 'Aziz,
Ya Wadud,
Ya Salaam.

Ya Matin, O You Who Are Ever Steadfast, Everlastingly Strong,
Ya Badi, O Skilful Creator
Ya Wasi, O All Encompassing One,
Ya 'Aziz, O Almighty, Most Dear,
Ya Wadud, O Infinitely Loving One,
Ya Salaam, O You Who Are Peace

And He/She has set upon the earth mountains standing firm
lest it should shake with you;
and rivers and roads, that you may guide yourselves,
and signs and means of orientation; for by the stars men find their way.
Is then He/She who creates like one who cannot create?
Will you not listen to counsel?
If you were to count the favors of God

never would you be able to compute them:
for God is Oft Forgiving, Most Merciful.
[16:15–18]

We have sent Our messengers with clear signs,
and through them We bestowed revelation and a balance
so that people might behave with justice;
and We sent down iron in which is awesome power
as well as many benefits for humankind,
that God might test who it is that will help unseen
Him / Her and His / Her messengers;
for truly, God is the Source of All Power, Almighty.
[57:25]

Be constant in your prayer
from the time when the sun has passed its zenith
until the darkness of night,
and always be mindful of its recitation at dawn:
for see how the recitation at dawn
is indeed witnessed by all that is holy.
And rise from your sleep and pray during part of the night,
as a free offering,
and your Sustainer may well raise you to a glorious station.
[17:78–79]

55. Al Wali, The Friend and Protector

Ya Wali, Ya Hafiz, Ya Nasir, Ya Samad, Ya Nur

O Friend and Protector,
Preserver of that which is Most Precious—
the Secret within these hearts
that You have written
on the Tablet
preserved and protected
for all Eternity—
help us to *keep our connection*
with the Source
of Our Sustenance,
of that Light
that allows us to see,
to read and know
what You have written,
Ya Nasir.
O Beloved Friend,
in Your Radiance
*we rest
and find tranquility.*

Ya Wali, O Friend and Protector,
Ya Hafiz, O Preserver and Protector,
Ya Nasir, O Helper,
Ya Samad, O Eternal, Satisfier of All Need,
Ya Nur, O You Who Are Light

*All the while God encompasses them
without their being aware of it.
Nay, but this is a sublime discourse,
inscribed on an imperishable tablet.*
[85:20–22]

*You alone do we worship and You alone do we ask for help.
Guide us on the straight path.*
[1:5–6]

God is enough for a Protector, and God is enough for a Helper.
[4:45]

*God knows all that enters within the earth
and all that comes forth out of it,
as well as all that descends from heaven
and all that ascends to it.
And God is with you wherever you may be
and sees well all that you do.
To God belongs the dominion of the heavens and the earth.
And all things return to God
who merges night into day and merges day into night
and knows completely the secrets of hearts.*
[57:4–6]

*And keep your connection, and remain conscious of God,
so that you might attain felicity.*
[3:200]

*Truly, my protector is God, who sent down this Book:
for it is He/She who protects the righteous.*
[7:196]

*The only protection comes from God, the True.
He/She is the best to reward and the best to give success.*
[18:44]

*Truly, in the remembrance of God
hearts find tranquility.*
[13:28]

56. Al Hamid, The One Worthy of Praise

Ya Hamid, Ya Ghani, Ya Haqq, Ya Wadud

O Most Praised One,
the One Worthy of All Praise,
You,
within us,
raise us
to Your stations—
held
in a breath
of knowing You
throughout
the cells of these structures,
created
to sing the song
of Your Love.
Your Book
of Exalted Power
comes to us
when You see
through us
and we catch
Your Glance
in the eyes
of these hearts.
To You belong
the east and the west,
all the heavens
and the earth,
these bodies
walking
Your Love,
Your Wisdom,

Your Generosity
through the fields
of being.
We dance
because You
have given us feet
and hearts
to hear the music
of the spheres
whose orbits
trace
eons of reckoning
in such perfection
we marvel
at Your Grace.
The Sun and the Moon
each traverse
their given paths;
the night cannot go
beyond the time of day.
Our parts we each
must play
upon this stage
of Your Bestowal.
You hold the keys
to recognition
of our deepest meaning,
for You are the Source
of our being,
the Truly Rich,
Worthy of All Praise.
You have given us
so many ways
to know You—
through our fingertips,
our toes,

and the hairs upon our heads,
this skin
that vibrates
with Your sound,
calling these hearts
to pause
and remember—
You are One,
and enfold us all
in Your Embrace,
the Living, the Loving.
Sometimes hidden
in the core of our hearts,
sometimes resplendent,
You play
this game of hide and seek
for the delight
of the finding—
Ya Wajid,
You who are Joy,
and love the laughter
that bubbles up
in the fountain
of sight—
not only throats,
but eyes and ears
You have given
everything, and tongues
to praise,
even though we
may not yet hear
all the manner
of voices.
"Arise and be joyful
all ye lands—
Your Lord has come.

Dance among the vines—
the harvest is near."
Always, the harvest is here—
it is not our hands
that have made it.
Will we not be grateful—
for these hands
that can reach
the ripened grapes
and catch the dates
falling from the palm trees
that stand waiting
to feed us?
All praise be to You,
Most Glorious,
Most Merciful,
You Who Are Truly Rich,
Ever Enriching us,
with Truth,
the Ever Living, Infinitely Loving,
Ya Hamid,
Ya Majid,
Ya Rahim,
Ya Ghani, Al Mughni,
Ya Haqq, Ya Wajid,
Al Ahad,
Ya Hayy,
Ya Wadud.

Ya Hamid, O You Who Are Worthy of All Praise,
Ya Majid, O Most Glorious, *Ya Rahim*, O Infinitely Merciful,
Ya Ghani, O You Who Are Truly Rich, *Al Mughni*, The Enricher,
Ya Haqq, O Truth, *Ya Wajid*, O Finder
(You who bring us ecstasy—*wajd*—when we find that we are found, by You, within You),
Al Ahad, the One, *Ya Hayy*, O Ever Living One,
Ya Wadud, O Infinitely Loving One

He/She loves them, and they love Him/Her.
[5:54]

Behold, it is a Book of Exalted Power:
no falsehood can ever approach it, before or behind it—
it is sent down by One who is Truly Wise, Worthy of All Praise.
[41:41–42]

To God belong the east and the west.
Wherever you turn, there is the Face of God.
Witness, God is All Encompassing, All Knowing.
[2:115]

The sun is not permitted to overtake the moon,
nor can the night go beyond the day,
but each moves easily in its lawful way.
[36:40]

To God belongs all that is in the heavens and on earth.
Truly, it is God who is Truly Rich,
the One to Whom All Praise Is Due!
[31:26]

The seven heavens acclaim His/Her limitless glory,
and the earth, and all that they contain;
and there is nothing that does not celebrate
His/Her immeasurable glory—
but you fail to grasp the manner of their glorifying Him/Her!
[17:44]

A Sign for them is the lifeless earth—
We bring it to life and out of it bring forth grain
of which they may eat.
And We produce there gardens with date-palms and vines,
and We cause springs to gush forth from within it,
that they may enjoy the fruits thereof.

It was not their hands that made this;
will they not then give thanks?
[36:33–35]

Make a joyful noise unto the Lord, all ye lands.
Serve the Lord with gladness:
come before His presence with singing.
Know ye that the Lord, He is God:
it is He that hath made us, and not we ourselves;
we are His people, and the sheep of His pasture.
Enter into His gates with thanksgiving,
and into His courts with praise:
be thankful unto Him, and bless His name.
For the Lord is Good; His mercy is Everlasting;
and His Truth endures to all generations.
[The Bible, Psalm 100: 1–5]

57. Al Muhsi, The One Who Keeps Account

Al Muhsi, Al Muqit, Al Qadir, Al Latif

Don't you know
that God knows
all that is hidden
and all we can see
and rectifies the balance continuously,
keeping account of the hairs
on our heads
even when they fall—
what we have eaten
embeds itself cell by cell.
Every night and every day
we are given moments
to see—
the angels are with us;
oceans of air
record every whisper
in droplets of dew
that resurrect with the dawn
and water
the garden beside our door.
To our right,
to our left,
the results of our actions
construct the palaces
or hovels
in which we live.
Are there windows?
How will the light enter?
The stars keep their courses
by Your Love.
Service purifies hearts

that we might rediscover
the center
and return to You
the pages we have written,
with golden ink glowing
and flowers growing
all around the borders
of our lives.

> *Al Muhsi*, The One Who Keeps Account,
> *Al Muqit*, The Nourisher,
> *Al Qadir*, The Determiner of Power,
> *Al Latif*, The Infinitely Subtle and Mysterious

> *He/She alone knows*
> *that which is beyond the reach of a created being's perception,*
> *and to none does He/She disclose any of the mysteries*
> *of His/Her own unfathomable knowledge,*
> *except to a messenger whom He/She was pleased to choose:*
> *and then He/She sends forth [the forces of heaven]*
> *to watch over him or her*
> *in whatever lies open before him/her*
> *and in what is beyond his/her ken—*
> *so as to make manifest*
> *that it is indeed their Sustainer's messages that these deliver:*
> *for it is He/She who encompasses all that is with them,*
> *just as He/She takes count, one by one, of everything.*
> [72:26–28]

> *Truly, there are Ever Watchful forces over you,*
> *noble, recording, aware of whatever you do.*
> [82:10–12]

> *And give full measure whenever you measure,*
> *and weigh with a balance that is true:*

this will be for your own good, and best in the end.
And do not follow anything of which you have no knowledge;
truly, hearing and sight and heart—all of them—
will be called to account for it.
[17:35–36]

And witness! We made the Temple²⁷ a goal
to which people might return again and again, and a sanctuary:
take, then, the place whereon Abraham stood as your place of prayer.
And thus did We command Abraham and Ishmael:
"Purify My Temple
for those who will walk around it,
and those who will abide near it in meditation,
and those who will bow down and prostrate themselves in prayer."
And, witness, Abraham prayed:
"O my Sustainer! Make this a land secure,
and grant its people fruitful sustenance—
those who have faith in God and the Day of Return."
[2:125–126]

On the Day when the soul and the angels will stand up in ranks:
none will speak but one to whom the Most Gracious will have given leave;
and will say what is right.
That will be the Day of Ultimate Truth:
whoever wills, then, let him or her take the path
that leads towards his/her Sustainer!
[78:38–39]

He/She covers the day with the night,
each swiftly following the other,
with the sun and the moon and the stars
in service to His/Her command:

---

27 "The Most Ancient Temple" [22:34], which signifies in locality, the Kaaba, and in subtlety, the heart of the human being.

oh, truly, His/Hers is all creation and all command.
Holy is God, the Cherisher and Sustainer of all the worlds!
[7:54]

The first and foremost of those who have left behind harm,
and of those who have sheltered and helped,
as well as those who follow them in beautiful striving—
God is well-pleased with them, and well-pleased are they with Him/Her.
And for them has He/She readied gardens
through which running waters flow,
therein to abide beyond the count of time: this is magnificent success!
[9:100]

58. Al Mubdi, The Originator

Ya Mubdi, Al Badi, Al Ba'ith, Al Baqi

O Originator
of all our thoughts—
the stem
of this brain
that flowers into Your Love—
everything we see and feel
begins with Your Knowing,
of us,
through us.
These heavens
and this earth,
all are tethered in Your stable.
We ride out
into Your storms
and find ourselves
remembered,
close,
under the blanket
of Your endearment,
You so love to be,
that You
vibrate through every bird's throat,
awakening us at dawn
with the song of the lark.
How could we imagine
power to be under our
aegis,
when we cannot call forth
a newborn babe
without Your creation?
You know all our comings and goings

through the waters of Your blessing.
Drop by drop
we come into being
and are swallowed by Your pouring.
Remember us back,
all the way to our Origin,
O You who love to be known,
welcome us Home
with the angels,
in the fragrant realm of lote trees
and abiding springs.

Ya Mubdi, O Originator, You Who Create Out of Nothing,
Al Badi, The Most Skilful Creator,
Al Ba'ith, The One Who Resurrects,
Al Baqi, The Forever Abiding One

"O my Sustainer!
You have indeed bestowed on me some power,
and have imparted to me some knowledge
of the inner meaning of that which occurs.
Originator of the heavens and the earth!
You are my Protector in this world and in the life to come:
let me die as one who has surrendered himself to You,
and unite me with the righteous!"
[12:101, prayer of the Prophet Joseph]

Are they then not aware of how God creates in the first instance,
and then brings it forth anew?
This, truly, is easy for God!
Say: "Go all over the earth and behold
how wondrously He/She originated creation:
even so will God bring into being the life after—
for, truly, over everything God is All Powerful!
[29:19–20]

Now, indeed, We create the human being out of the essence of clay,
and then We cause him/her to remain
as a drop of sperm in [the womb's] firm keeping,
and then We create out of the drop of sperm a connecting cell,
and then We create out of the connecting cell an embryonic mass,
and then We create within the embryonic mass bones,
and then We clothe the bones with flesh—
and then We bring this into being as a new creation:
how holy is God, the best of Creators!
And then, behold! after all this, you are destined to die;
and then, behold, you shall be raised from the dead
on the Day of Resurrection.
And, indeed, We have created above you seven heavenly paths;
and never are We unmindful of any part of Our creation.
[23:12–17]

Who is it that guides you in the midst of the deep darkness of land and sea,
and sends forth the winds as a glad tiding of His/Her coming grace?
Can there be any divine power besides God?
Sublimely exalted is God far beyond anything
by which people may attempt to describe His/Her divinity.
Or who is it that originates creation, and then brings it forth anew?
And who is it that provides you with sustenance out of heaven and earth?
Can there be any divine power besides God?
[27:63–64]

Now as for those who have attained to righteousness—
what of those who have attained to righteousness:
amid fruitful lote-trees,
and flowering acacias, and sheltering shade, and waters gushing,
and abundant fruit, never-failing and never out of reach.
[56:27–33]

Truly, they who attain to faith and do rightful deeds of wholeness
shall have gardens through which running waters flow—
that triumph most great!

Truly, your Sustainer's grasp is exceedingly strong!
Behold, it is He/She who creates in the first instance,
and He/She will bring him/her forth anew.
And He/She alone is Truly Forgiving, All Embracing in His/Her Love,
Sovereign of the throne of Sublime Majesty.
[85:11–14]

59. Al Muʿid, The Restorer

Ya Muʿid, Ya ʿAdl, Ya Muqsit

A new day
is dawning,
and the dross
burns away
in the Light
of Love's fire,
purifying
and restoring hearts
that have been wounded.
Ya Muʿid,
You know
how to care for us,
when we recoil
in fear,
tightly wound
around our core
in defense against
that which we have felt,
we have known,
to harm us—
You relax again
these bones,
these muscles and sinews,
to breathe in
Your Grace
that washes us afresh,
reminding us
that You are Greater
than any concern
and have the Power
to Guard and Preserve,

Ya Wakil, Ya Hafiz,
Ya Wadud, Ya Wali,
O You who Love
to Rectify the Balance,
to smoothe the tangles
of our being,
that we might sing
again Your Praises
in these melted hearts
that warm with Your Seeing
of us, and through us,
knowing Your Ever Living Love,
that strengthens us
in resolve
to do Your bidding—
Your urging
to the Most Beautiful,
the Most Gracious,
the Most Compassionate,
Mercy of Mercies,
from within these springs
of Your Justice and Rectitude.
Ya 'Adl, Ya Muqsit,
Ya Salaam.

Ya Mu'id, O You Who Restore,
Ya Wakil, O Guardian of All Our Affairs,
Ya Hafiz, O Preserver,
Ya Wadud, O Infinitely Loving One,
Ya Wali, O Friend and Protector,
Ya 'Adl, O Most Just,
Ya Muqsit, O You Who Love to Rectify the Balance,
Ya Salaam, O You Who Are Peace and Inspire Peace within Us

Say: "It is God who creates originally,
and then brings it forth renewed."
[10:34]

If a wound has touched you,
be sure a similar wound has touched others.
Such days We give to people by turns:
that God may know those who have faith,
and that He/She may take to Himself/Herself
witnesses to the truth from among you.
And God does not love those who do harm;
and that God might render pure of all dross
those who have attained to faith,
and bring to nothing those who turn away from the Truth—
do you reckon that you could enter the Garden
unless God has recognized your striving,
and recognized your patience in adversity?
[3:140–142]

In the Name of God, the Infinitely Compassionate and Most Merciful:
Say, "I seek refuge with the Lord of the Dawn
from the mischief of created things;
from the evil of Darkness as it overspreads;
from the harmfulness of those who blow on knots;[28]
and from the harm of the envious one as he or she envies."
[113:1–5]

In the Name of God, the Infinitely Compassionate and Most Merciful:
Say, "I seek refuge with the Sustainer of humankind,
the Sovereign of humankind,
the God of humankind,
from the mischief of the slinking whisperer

---

28 Those who cast spells; those who spread constriction, who exacerbate difficulties.

*who whispers in the hearts of human beings
among jinns and among humankind."*
[114:1–6]

*Truly: all who surrender their whole being to God,
and do good, shall have their reward with their Sustainer;
these need have no fear, neither shall they grieve.*
[2:112]

*Those who have faith
and who have turned away from evil
and who strive in the Way of God
with their wealth and their lives
have the highest rank in God's sight,
and it is they who gain felicity!
Their Sustainer gives them glad tidings
of the Compassion that flows from Him,
and of His abundant pleasure,
and of the gardens for them, of enduring bliss,
there to dwell forever.
Truly, in God's Presence is a mighty recompense!*
[9:20–22]

60. Al Muhyi, The One Who Gives Life
& 61. Al Mumit, The One Who Takes Life

Ya Muhyi, Al Mumit, Ya Rauf, Ya Karim, Ya Wadud

O You Who Give Life,
O You Who Take Life
into Your Own Hands,
we have no worries
about our end,
when we know
it is to You *we*
are returning.
You, Most Gracious,
Most Kind,
Most Generous
and Sustaining,
even through
all our travails,
You never leave us,
for *Your Mercy Overwhelms*
Your stringency.
Drinking deep
of Your Love,
we leave our
bitter dregs
behind—
they simply
fall away
as we rise
in Your Light,
called Home
to the Heavens.
And in a moment,
even the dregs

may be transformed
and become again
a fertile greenness,
for succulent
green and purple grapes,
heavy on the vine.
Your fertility
is renewed
by a single
breath, and
we are poured
again into
vessels for new
wine—
white or red,
golden
in these glasses,
or held
to age
and ripen
in these skins
that walk
Your Love around.

Ya Muhyi, O Giver of Life, *Al Mumit*, The Giver of Death,
Ya Rahman, O Infinitely Gracious and Compassionate One,
Ya Rauf, O Most Kind, *Ya Karim*, O Infinitely Generous One,
Ya Wadud, O Infinitely Loving One

*Say: "O humankind! Truly, I am a messenger of God, to all of you,
unto whom the dominion over the heavens and the earth belongs!
There is no deity except Him/Her;
He/She grants life and grants death."*
[7:158]

Say: "Truly, my prayer, and all my acts of worship,
and my living and my dying are for God alone,
the Sustainer of all worlds."
[6:162]

It is God who sends forth the winds, so that they raise a cloud—
whereupon He/She spreads it over the skies as He/She wills,
and causes it to break so that you see rain emerge from within it:
and as soon as He/She causes it to fall
upon whomever He/She wills of His/Her servants—
see how they rejoice, even though a short while ago,
before it was sent down upon them, they had abandoned all hope!
Behold, then, these signs of God's grace—
how He/She gives life to the earth after it had been lifeless!
Truly, the same it is who can bring those who are dead back to life:
for He/She has the power to will anything!
[30:48–50]

"Establish for us what is good, in this world as well as hereafter—
see how we have turned towards You!"
God's word came: "With my Stringency I try whom I will,
but even so, My Mercy encompasses everything.
And so I shall confer it upon those who are regardful of Me,
and share of their abundance, and have faith in Our signs."
[7:156]

Have you ever considered that which you emit?
Is it you who create it—or are We the source of its creation?
We have decreed that death shall be with you:
but there is nothing to prevent Us from changing the nature of your existence
and bringing you into being in a new manner unknown to you.
And you must be aware of the miracle
of your coming into being to begin with—
why, then, do you not reflect?
Have you ever considered the seed which you cast upon the soil?
Is it you who cause it to grow—or are We the cause of its growth?
[56:58–64]

And We have sent the fertilizing winds,
and We send down water from the skies for you to drink of it—
you are not the keepers of its source—
for, behold, it is We—We alone—who grant life and grant death,
and it is We alone who shall remain after all else will have passed away.
And well do We know all those who lived before you
and those who will come after you;
and, behold, it is your Sustainer who will gather them all together:
truly, He/She is All Wise, All Knowing!
[15:22–25]

Oh, truly, unto God belongs all that is in the heavens and on earth!
Oh, truly, God's promise always comes true—
but most of them know it not!
He/She alone grants life and grants death;
and unto Him/Her will you all be brought back.
[10:55–56]

We come from God and to Him/Her we shall return.
[2:156]

62. Al Hayy, The Ever Living
& 63. Al Qayyum, The Eternal, Self-Subsisting Source

Ya Hayy, Ya Qayyum, Ya Rahman, Ya Wadud

O You who are Ever Living
and guard us with Your Grace,
the angels know
Your agelessness,
for time stops in Your Presence.
We are ever young
when we enter
the vortex of Your Love,
right hand raised
to catch Your rain,
we join Your flowing
when another hand bestows
without counting
the giving.
Ya Qayyum,
You keep us rooted
in Eternity,
steadfast,
one foot planted
on this earth,
head raised
in Your heavens;
round and round we go
in this dance of day and night.
Sunflowers turn to you
each moment of the day.
New breaths
take on new shapes—
O Ever Living One,
how much You must love life,

that every fraction of a second
countless new beings spring forth!
Life stems
from Your Eternal Smile.
As drops of rain,
we fall from Your kiss,
and within the oyster shell
of this world become pearls
through the action of Your Grace.
This ocean of being keeps surging;
Your whales love Your Ocean,
and Your Ocean loves Your whales,
lilting their bodies with its songs.
The story keeps unfolding, flowing
forth and back with Your Love.
Ya Hayy,
Ya Qayyum,
Ya Rahman,
Ya Wadud.

Ya Hayy, O Ever Living One,
Ya Qayyum, O Eternal, Upright, Self-Subsisting Source,
Ya Rahman, O Infinitely Compassionate One,
Ya Wadud, O Infinitely Loving One

God—there is no god but Hu,
the Ever Living, the Eternal, Self-Subsisting Source.
[3:2]

It is out of His/Her Compassion
that He/She has made for you night and day—
that you may rest within it, and that you may seek His/Her Grace,
and so that you might be grateful.
[28:73]

Say, O you, My servants who have come to faith:
"Be conscious of your Sustainer:
good is for those who persevere in doing good in this world.
Spacious is God's earth!
Those who patiently persevere
will truly receive a reward beyond measure!"
[39:10]

And so, place your trust in the Living One who dies not,
and celebrate His/Her limitless glory and praise.
[25:58]

Hu knows all that is before them and all that is hidden from them,
but they cannot encompass Him/Her with their knowledge.
All faces shall be humbled
before the Ever Living, the Self-Subsisting, Eternal Fount of Being:
hopeless indeed will be the one who carries corruption,
but the one who acts rightly and has faith
need have no fear of being wronged or ever diminished.
[20:110–112]

It is God who has made for you the earth as a resting place
and the sky as a canopy
and has given you shapes and made your shapes beautiful
and has provided for you sustenance of pure and good things—
such is God, your Sustainer.
So Glory to God, the Sustainer of all the Worlds!
He/She is the Ever Living: there is no god but He/She.
Call upon Him/Her, sincere in your faith in Him/Her.
Praise be to God, Sustainer of all the Worlds!
[40:64–65]

For it is He/She who has brought into being gardens—
both the cultivated ones and those growing wild—
and the date-palm, and fields bearing all manner of produce,
and the olive, and the pomegranate:

all resembling one another and yet so different!
Eat of their fruit when it ripens,
and contribute appropriate portions on harvest day.
[6:141]

He/She is the Instructor of the two places of sunrise,
and the Instructor of the two places of sunset.
Then which of your Sustainer's blessings will you deny?
He/She has given freedom to the two great bodies of water
so that they might meet:
yet between them is a threshold which they cannot cross.
Then which of your Sustainer's blessings will you deny?
Out of these come pearls and coral.
Then which of your Sustainer's blessings will you deny?
And His/Hers are the ships sailing smoothly, lofty as mountains,
through the seas.
Then which of your Sustainer's blessings will you deny?
[55:17–25]

In the flowering meadows of the gardens
will be those who have come to faith
and have done the deeds of wholeness and reconciliation:
all that they might desire shall they have with their Sustainer:
this, this is the magnificent abundance—
that of which God gives the glad tidings
to those of His/Her servants who come into faith
and do healthful deeds of wholeness.
[42:22–23]

64. Al Wajid, The Finder

Ya Wajid, Ya Karim, Ya Wadud

O You Who Find us,
*every morning
and evening seeking Your Face,
who allow neither business nor trade
to distract us* from our goal,
we submerge into You
and burst like whales
upon the horizon, so full of joy,
when rainbows arc through the sun
kissed by the rain.
Male and female You have created,
to give us a semblance of Your Love,
and the fertile greenness
that erupts upon the hills in Your Light.
Yes, sometimes we wander,
yet through the corner of an eye,
can catch a glimpse of You,
and know Your promise is true—
"*Always, I am with you.*"
A Treasure
that was Hidden,
You find us ever anew,
You who are the ecstasy
of Being,
Ya Wajid,
Ya Karim,
Ya Wadud.

Ya Wajid, O You Who Find Us,
Ya Karim, O Most Generous One,
Ya Wadud, O Infinitely Loving One

*For, truly, We found [Job] full of patience in adversity:
how excellent a servant, who, behold, would always turn to Us!*
[38:44]

*In the houses which God has allowed to be raised
so that His/Her Name shall be remembered in them,
there are those who praise His/Her limitless glory
morning and evening—
those whom neither business nor striving after gain
can turn from the remembrance of God,
and from constancy in prayer, and from charity:
who are filled with awe
of the Day on which all hearts and eyes will be transformed,
who only hope that God will give them recompense
in accordance with the best of their actions,
and give them even more out of His/Her blessing:
for God grants sustenance to whom He/She wills,
beyond all reckoning.*
[24:36–38]

*Remember Our servant David,
he who was endowed with inner strength:
for he always turned to Us.
It was We who made the hills declare Our praises
in unison with him
at nightfall and at break of day.
And the birds gathered: all with him did turn.
We strengthened his dominion
and gave him wisdom and sound judgment in speech and decisions.*
[38:17–20]

*O human beings! Behold,
We have created you all out of a male and a female,
and have made you into nations and tribes,
so that you might come to know one another.
Truly, the noblest of you in the sight of God*

is the one who is most deeply conscious of Him / Her.
Behold, God is All Knowing, All Aware.
[49:13]

Those who attain to faith and do rightful deeds of wholeness and health
We shall bring into gardens through which running waters flow,
therein to abide beyond the count of time;
there shall they have spouses pure
and We shall bring them unto sheltering happiness abounding.
[4:57]

Witness! Your Sustainer inspired the angels
to convey His / Her message to the faithful:
"I am with you!"
[8:12]

"I was a Hidden Treasure, and I so loved to be known
that I created the two worlds, seen and Unseen,
in order that My Treasure of Generosity and Loving-kindness
might be known."
[*Hadith Qudsi*]

65. Al Majid, The Magnificent, Tremendous in Glory

Al Majid, Al Rahim, Al Ghafur, An Nur, Ar Razzaq, Al Wadud

Tremendous,
in Mercy
and Forgiveness,
You send Your angels
with the breeze,
upon Your clouds
to remind us
always of Your Blessing.
Jonah was overwhelmed,
swallowed by Your Wisdom,
and granted subsistence
founded on Your shores of Grace,
still kissed by the Ocean,
every day.
We tremble
with the weight
of Your Word,
and yet You strengthen
us with mountains of giving,
companions of light
who can bear
the Brilliance—
stars of Truth
in Your diadem
encircling our planet,
they host us at Your table,
even as Jesus
reminds us—
in Your Presence
a feast is always revealed:
"Continuously, I am sending it."

And our hearts, too,
like Jonah's
become light
with your Love,
and our people,
our bodies, our selves
are spared
the tribulation
we might have set upon them
through our ignorance
and haste.
Ya Majid,
all praise be to You,
Sustainer of All Worlds,
Ya Nur,
Ar Razzaq,
Al Wadud.

Al Majid, The Magnificent in Glory,
Ar Rahim, The Infinitely Merciful,
Al Ghafur, The Oft Forgiving, *An Nur*, The Light,
Ar Razzaq, The Best of Providers,
Al Wadud, The Infinitely Loving One

*Limitless is He/She in His/Her glory, and sublimely exalted
far beyond anything to which people may ascribe a share in His/Her divinity!*
[10:18]

*And remember him of the great fish—when he went off in wrath,
thinking that We had no power over him!
But then he cried out in the deep darkness of distress: "There is no deity but You!
Limitless are You in Your glory! Truly, I have done wrong!"
And so We responded unto him and delivered him from distress:
for thus do We deliver all who have faith.*
[21:87–88]

Clearly does He/She spell out these messages unto people of inner knowing:
for, truly, in the alternating of night and day,
and in all that God has created in the heavens and on earth
there are messages indeed for people who are conscious of Him/Her!
[10:5–6]

The people of Jonah—when they came to have faith,
We removed from them the suffering of disgrace in the life of this world,
and allowed them to enjoy their life during the time apportioned to them.
[10:98]

Say: "Who is it that provides you with sustenance out of heaven and earth,
or who is it that has full power over hearing and sight?
And who is it that brings forth the living out of that which is dead,
and brings forth the dead out of that which is alive?
And who is it that governs all that exists?"
And they will answer: "God."
Say, then: "Won't you, then, become conscious of Him/Her—
seeing that He/She is God, your Sustainer, the Ultimate Truth?"
[10:31–32]

The faithful are those
whose hearts tremble with awe whenever God is mentioned,
and whose faith is strengthened
whenever His/Her signs are conveyed to them.
[8:2]

Said Jesus, the son of Mary: "O God, our Sustainer!
Send down upon us a repast from heaven:
it shall be an ever-recurring feast for us—
for the first and the last of us—and a sign from You.
And provide us our sustenance,
for You are the Best of Providers!"
God answered: "Truly, I am always sending it down to you."
[5:114–115]

*He / She alone is Truly Forgiving, All Embracing in His / Her Love,
in Sublime Magnificence Enthroned.*
[85:14–15]

66. Al Wahid, The One, The Unique
& 67. Al Ahad, The One, All Inclusive In Your Unity

Ya Ahad, Ya Wahid, Ya Sami, Ya Wadud

O You Who Hear and Understand All Tongues
forgive us,
for all the moments of misspeaking,
for taking another's name in vain,
for riling defenses.
You have told us
to *speak only with the most beautiful urgings.*
From the depths of our souls
we long to communicate
with You within each other,
for You are nowhere absent.
We know this to be true
when our hearts are awake:
"*I am with you.*"
Ever Present Source
of our own meaning,
how can we deny
or turn away from anyone
who holds Your Precious Essence?
When we are shy or disgruntled,
help us to forget the self
that would separate,
for in You we know oneness.
Ya Ahad—
the Only One, Al Wahid—
You Who Join Us All in Oneness,
Al Wujud al Karim,
the Most Generous Bestower of Being,
We belong to You,
for we are of You,

and *to You we shall return,*
in every moment,
with every breath
passing through these hearts
You keep filling with Love,
Ya Wadud,
even as light fills the sky
at dawn and darkness vanishes.
There are no corners to Your Loving.
Wash us clear with Your Love,
Ya Quddus, Ya Ahad, Ya Wadud.

Ya Ahad, O You Who Join Us All in Oneness,
Ya Wahid, O Only One,
Ya Wadud, O Infinitely Loving One,
Ya Sami, O All Hearing One, You Who Understand All Tongues,
Ya Samad, Ever Present and Eternal Source,
Al Wujud al Karim, The Most Generous Bestower of Being,
Ya Quddus, O Most Holy and Pure

Say, "Hu is God, the One;
God, Hu, the Eternal Source of Subsistence."
[112:1]

O you who have come to faith!
Let no men look down upon other men—
it may be that those are better than they;
and let no women look down upon other women—
it may be that those are better than they.
And neither shall you speak ill of one another,
nor insult one another with shameful names:
harmful is all name-calling after one has come to have faith.
[49:11]

Say: "I am but a man like yourselves;
the revelation has come to me that your God is the Only God, the One.
And so, whoever looks forward to meeting his or her Sustainer,
let him or her do rightful deeds of wholeness and reconciliation,
and let him/her not ascribe unto anyone or anything
a share in the worship due to his/her Sustainer!"
[18:110]

Invite to the way of your Sustainer
with wisdom and beautiful urging.
[16:125]

And your creation or your resurrection
is in no other way than as a single soul:
for God is the One Who Hears and Sees all things.
[31:28]

Say: "I am only a warner; and there is no deity whatever but God, the One,
the One Who Irresistibly Holds Sway over all that exists,
the Sustainer of the heavens and the earth and all that is between them,
the Almighty, the All Forgiving!"
[38:65–66]

And anyone who honors the symbols set up by God—
truly, these derive their value
from the God-consciousness within the heart.
In that God-consciousness you shall find benefits
until a determined time is fulfilled,
and its goal and end is the Most Ancient Temple[29]...
And always bear in mind your God is the One and Only God:
and so, surrender yourselves to Hu.
And give the glad tiding of God's acceptance to all who are humble—
all those whose hearts tremble with awe whenever God is mentioned,

---

29 See note 26 (p. 174).

and all who patiently bear whatever ill befalls them,
and all who are constant in prayer and spend on others
out of the sustenance We have provided for them.
[22:32–35]

And Your God is the Only One—there is no divinity but Hu
who is the Infinitely Compassionate, the Infinitely Merciful.
[2:163]

Witness! Your Sustainer inspired the angels
to convey His/Her message to the faithful:
"I am with you!"
[8:12]

And to Him/Her will you all return.
[28:88]

Ask forgiveness of your Sustainer and turn to Him/Her:
for truly, my Sustainer is Infinitely Merciful and Infinitely Loving.
[11:90]

68. As Samad, The Eternal, Satisfier of All Need

Ya Samad, Ya Wajid, Ya Raqib, Ya Salaam, Ya Wadud

O You Who are Eternal,
Ever Present Source
of our deepest being,
You who welcome us Home,
we reach into You
and find ourselves
held
in Your Eternal Peace.
When we are lost,
You re-discover us;
when we are in need,
You know,
for You are the Satisfier
of any need arising
throughout these worlds.
Your ambush catches us
in the net of Your Love,
and we adore Your Face
reflected in the hills
and seas,
the flowers, the birds, the trees.
Eternal, Self-Subsistent,
rectifying the balance
and searching
out our hearts,
You are Ever Present
and lift our vision
with Your Eye
that is Ever Watchful,
Ya Raqib.
Behind everything we do and are,

resting in Your Self,
we rest, too, when we remember
You and dive deeply
into the Ocean of Your Love.

Ya Samad, O Eternal, Ever Present Satisfier of All Need,
Ya Wajid, O You Who Find us,
Ya Raqib, O Ever Watchful One,
Ya Salaam, O You Who Are Peace,
Ya Wadud, O Infinitely Loving One

Say, "Hu is God, the One;
God, Hu, the Eternal Satisfier of All Need.
[112:1–2]

God—there is no god but Hu,
the Ever Living, the Self-Subsisting Source of Being.
Step by step He/She has sent down to you this Book,
setting forth the truth which confirms
whatever remains of earlier revelations:
for it is He/She who earlier bestowed from on high
the Torah and the Gospel, as a guidance to humankind,
and it is He/She who has bestowed the standard for discernment.
[3:2–4]

He/She separates what is harmful from that which is good.
[3:179]

Celebrate your Sustainer's limitless glory and praise Him/Her,
and be of those who prostrate themselves in adoration,
and worship your Sustainer until nearness comes to you.
[15:98–99]

He/She guides to Himself/Herself all who turn to Him/Her—
those who have faith

and whose hearts find tranquility in the remembrance of God—
for, truly, in the remembrance of God hearts find rest.
[13:27–28]

69. Al Qadir, The Pourer of Power
& 70. Al Muqtadir, The Determiner

Ya Qadir, Ya Muqtadir, Ya 'Adl

O You who measure all
in the most beautiful proportion,
teach us Your Wisdom
to know
what to do when,
how much or how little.
May we water the roses,
not the thorns,
except enough to protect
the tender branches
and feed the camels,
and goats
who find there their sustenance.
So well You have ordered
this creation;
let us not overstep our bounds
with pride
assuming we have power
to override Your laws
of nature and their
recompense,
when we step over
each other
to gain more
of anything in our rush
for gold.
Let us not sell our souls for such a little price—
when You have poured
such elegance and grace
into these vessels of Your Love—

what a Treasure You have measured
into these hearts!
We are in awe
of the power that can come
to us, even in the night,
when we are listening,
even as Muhammad
in the cave—
hearts melt in Your Light.
The dross flows away
and we are bright
in the Truth of Your Giving,
always of the Best—
may we recognize it in each other
and belittle no one,
honoring all that You have made,
for You are Al Muqtadir,
the Supreme in Power
and in Love,
and can intimate Yourself
into the smallest of us.
Atoms whirl within Your Grace.
Your energy keeps us going,
searching, and knowing
Your inspiration
upon the wings of the angels
singing in the dawn.

Ya Qadir, O Pourer of Power,
Ya Muqtadir, O Supremely Powerful Determiner of Existence,
Ya 'Adl, O You Who Are Completely Just

He/She is the Sustainer of the worlds.
He/She established the mountains standing high above it

and bestowed blessings on the earth,
and measured all things there to give them nourishment in due proportion.
[41:9–10]

Have We not created you out of an infinitesimal fluid,
which We then let remain in the womb's firm keeping for a determined term?
Thus have We determined the nature of the human being,
and felicitous indeed is Our power to determine!
[77:20–23]

"O my people! measure and weigh justly
and don't deprive people of what is rightfully theirs;
and don't act harmfully on earth, spreading corruption.
That which rests with God is best for you
if you would have faith!"
[11:85–86, saying of the Prophet Shu'ayb]

And He/She has made in service to you as a gift from Him/Her
all that is in the heavens and on earth:
witness, truly, in that are signs for those who reflect.
Tell those who have faith to forgive
those who do not consider the coming of the Days of God:
it is for Him/Her to recompense each People
according to what they have earned.
If anyone does a righteous deed it is to his/her own benefit;
if he/she does harm it works against his/her own soul.
In the end you will all be brought back to your Sustainer.
[45:13–15]

Are, then, they not aware that God,
who has created the heavens and the earth
and never been wearied by their creation,
has the power to bring the dead back to life?
Yes, truly, He has the power to will anything!
[46:33]

Truly, in the Messenger of God you have a beautiful standard
for anyone whose hope is in God and the Day of Return
and who remembers God unceasingly.
[33:21]

Whatever is in the heavens and on earth
declares the praises and glory of God:
to Hu belongs all sovereignty and to Hu belongs all praise,
and Hu has power over all things.
[64:1]

And to everyone who is conscious of God,
God always prepares a way of emergence,
and provides for him/her in ways he/she could never imagine;
and for everyone who places trust in God, God is sufficient.
For God will surely accomplish His/Her purpose:
truly, for all things has God appointed an appropriate measure.
[65:2–3]

In the Name of God, the Infinitely Compassionate and Infinitely Merciful:
We have indeed revealed this during the Night of Power.[30]
And what will explain to you what the Night of Power is?
The Night of Power is better than a thousand months.
Within it the angels descend bearing divine inspiration
by God's permission upon every mission:
Peace! . . . This until the rise of dawn!
[97:1–5]

---

30 The night during which the Prophet Muhammad received the first revelation of the Quran is referred to as the "Night of Power". Historically, it is recognized as one of the last ten nights of the month of Ramadan, probably the 27th. Yet, a "Night of Power" may arrive any moment, a night when inspiration and closeness with one's Sustainer are present, so one is ever watchful for the arrival of that infinite blessing.

71. Al Muqaddim, The Expediter
& 72. Al Mu'akhkhir, The Delayer

Ya Muqaddim, Al Mu'akhkhir, As Samad, Ya Haqq

Ya Muqaddim, Al Mu'akhkhir, As Samad,
O You, from before the before,
Who move us forward,
and after the end
keep us halted
in Your School
until we come
to know
all the forces
of Your Power,
every hour
attending us,
supporting
and defending us,
even in the face
of these strange selves
we have not yet
come to understand.
So many lessons
You teach us
on this pilgrimage
Home to You.
We wander
through many lands
with ice and snow
and sun
and palm-trees
waving in Your breeze,
welcoming us
to the Spring

that eternally flows,
"Zam, zam!"
"Stop!"
"Drink of My Abundance
and carry
My Water
to those who are thirsting."
Ya Muqaddim,
help us to
overcome all our obstacles;
delaying us,
O Mu'akhkhir,
when in Your Wisdom
You see
that we need
a pause
to reflect,
to remember,
who we are.
O Solace
of the world,
of hearts
and souls
and spirits
encapsulated in forms,
You melt
us into
Timelessness
where there
is
no "forward"
and no "back,"
the placeless
place
of
As Samad,

Eternal, Infinite,
where all that is is Real,
is You,
Ya Haqq,
Ya Karim,
Ya Wadud.
Subhanallahi
'amma yushrikun,
Wal hamdulillahi
Rabbil 'Alameen,
Ya Rahman, Ya Rahim,
Ya Haqq, Ya Wadud.

Ya Muqaddim, O Expediter, *Al Mu'akhkhir,* The One Who Delays,
As Samad, The Eternal, Satisfier of All Needs,
Ya Haqq, O Truth, *Ya Karim,* O Infinitely Generous One,
Ya Wadud, O Infinitely Loving One,
Subahanallahi 'amma yushrikun, Glory be to God,
who is far beyond anything by which they may try to define Him/Her,
Wal hamdulillahi, Rabbil 'Alameen, And all praise belongs to God,
Sustainer of All Worlds,
Ya Rahman, O Infinitely Compassionate One,
Ya Rahim, O Infinitely Merciful One,
Ya Haqq, O Truth, *Ya Wadud,* O Infinitely Loving One

He/She is the Best Protector and the Best to Give Support.
[8:40]

He/She grants them respite until a determined moment:
but when the end of their term approaches,
they can neither delay it by a single moment, nor can they hasten it.
[16:61]

Say: "It is God who guides to the Truth."
[10:35]

*For, when We assigned to Abraham the site of this Temple,[31]
We said to him: "Do not attribute divinity to anything beside Me!"—
and: "Purify My Temple for those who will walk around it,
and those who will stand before it,
and those who will bow down in prostration."
And so, proclaim the pilgrimage to all people:
they will come to you on foot and on every kind of fast conveyance,
coming from every far-away place,
so that they might experience much that shall be of benefit to them,
and that they might glorify God's name.*
[22:26–28]

*Say: "This is my way:
based on understanding through conscious insight,
I am calling to God—I and those who follow me."
And say: "Limitless is God in His/Her glory;
and never will I be of those who attribute divinity
to anything beside Him/Her!"*
[12:108]

*Truly, God is Most Powerful, Almighty, Most Dear!
God chooses message-bearers from among the angels
as well as from among human beings,
for, behold, God is All Hearing, All Seeing:
He/She knows all that lies open before them
and all that is hidden from them—
for all things return [home] to God.
O you who have attained to faith!
Bow and prostrate yourselves, and adore your Sustainer,
and do good, so that you might attain to a happy state!
And strive hard in God's cause
with all the striving that is due to Him/Her:
it is He/She who has chosen you,*

---

31 See note 26 (p. 174).

and has placed no difficulty on you in religion,
the religion of your forefather Abraham.
It is He/She who has named you—in bygone times as well as in this—
"those who have surrendered themselves to God,"
so that the Messenger might bear witness to the Truth before you,
and that you might bear witness to it before all humankind.
And so, be constant in prayer, and render the purifying charity,
and hold fast unto God.
He/She is your Sovereign Protector:
and how excellent is this Sovereign Protector,
and how excellent this Giver of Succor!
[22:74–78]

Behold, We have given you the Source of Abundance.
[108:1]

God is He/She other than whom there is no god,
the Sovereign, the Holy One, the Source of Peace,
the Inspirer of Faith, the Preserver of Security,
the Exalted in Might, the Compelling, the Supreme:
Glory to God, who is subtly amazing,
far beyond anything by which they may try to define Him/Her.
[59:22–23]

Truly, those who have faith and do righteous deeds
their Sustainer will guide by means of their faith:
beneath them will flow rivers in Gardens of Bliss.
There they will call out: "Glory to You, O God!"
and they will be answered with the greeting, "Peace!"
And the completion of their cry will be:
"Praise be to God, the Cherisher and Sustainer of all the Worlds!"
[10:10]

73. Al Awwal, The First
& 74. Al Akhir, The Last

Ya Awwal, Ya Akhir, Ya Warith

O Writer, O Painter, O Sculptor, O Artist
of the Most Beautiful Beauty,
we are in awe
of all You display before us,
the First to unfold being,
the Last after all else is done,
the Inheritor of Everything
we are and witness,
we trust in Your utter Beneficence,
from which we drink
every day,
and the knowledge
You have inspired in us
that we return to You,
for we are Yours—
with every breath, you claim us—
how can we imagine separation,
when our very fingertips
carry Your signature
of infinite diversity
and flexibility of power,
the beauty of patterns
from Your unfolding.
O Creator,
within this Beauty
we breathe
and discover
every moment
another vista
of the expressions

of Your Face,
for surely,
wherever we turn,
You are with us.
When we call out in need,
You may not grant just
what we are asking,
but *always You answer
something of our prayer.*
O You Who Always Respond,
You are the First to awaken us,
and the Last to bring us to rest.
Ya Awwal, Ya Akhir, Ya Warith,
Ya Khaliq, Ya Bari, Ya Mussawir.
You are the Best of Inheritors.
*Everything is perishing,
except the Face of God.*

Ya Awwal, O You Who Are the First,
Ya Akhir, O You Who Are Last,
Ya Warith, O Inheritor of All,
Ya Khaliq, O Creator, *Ya Bari*, O Evolver,
Ya Mussawir, O Shaper of Form

*God is the First and the Last, the Manifest and the Hidden,
and knows completely all things.
It is God Who created the heavens and the earth in six aeons
and is firmly settled on the Throne of Power.*
[57:3]

*Say: "My Sustainer has but urged the doing of what is rightful;
and He/She wants you to put your whole being into every act of worship,
and to call Him/Her, sincere in your faith in Him/Her alone.*

As it was He/She who brought you into being in the beginning,
so also to Him/Her will you return."
[7:29]

Wherever you turn there is the Face of God.
[2:115]

And always does He/She give you something
out of what you may be asking of Him/Her;
and should you try to count God's blessings,
you could never compute them.
[14:34]

In the Name of God, the Infinitely Compassionate and Most Merciful:
By the glorious morning light,
and by the night when it is still,
Your Sustainer has not forgotten you,
nor is He/She displeased with you:
for, truly, that which comes after
will be better for you than that which came before!
And soon your Sustainer will give you
that with which you will be content.
Didn't He/She find you an orphan, and shelter you?
Didn't He/She find you wandering, and guide you?
Didn't He/She find you in need and satisfy your need?
So, do not be harsh with orphans,
nor turn away someone who asks something of you,
but continually declare the blessings of your Sustainer.
[93:1–11]

Everything is perishing, except the Face of God.
[28:88]

75. Az Zahir, The Manifest
& 76. Al Batin, The Hidden

Az Zahir, Al Batin, Ya Rauf, Ya Karim

Human Reality—
Hu,
how could we exist
without Your Graciousness?
Chivalry—
who is more chivalrous than You?
Freedom—
in Your Expansive Breath,
and even in constriction,
You create doorways
for our soaring
into Your Presence.
Miraj is not
"above,"
or "below,"
but everywhere apparent,[32]
even in Your most hidden chambers
where we are closest to You—
these hearts that know Your movement
with every beat;
You press the notes of our existence,
strumming us in harmony

---

[32] Muhammad said, "Don't see me as superior to Jonah, the son of Amittai, because he lived his *mi'raj* (ascension) at the bottom of the sea, within the belly of the fish, while I made my *mi'raj* beyond the seven heavens. Never see me as superior to him because of this!"
 To consider Truth as bound to heights or depths is to assume that Truth could be bound to a location.
~*Rumi's Sun, the Teachings of Shams of Tabriz*, p. 319, regarding the *hadith* related by Ibn Abbas.

with You,
O Most Kind,
Most Generous and Noble,
Most Forbearing and Resilient!
Seven sisters cluster close,
while the pole Star beckons.
Your Power is always for the Good,
Ya Zahir al Batin,
Ya Karim, Ya Wadud.
Out and in,
in and out,
You breathe us.
Your Hand draws the pictures we paint,
the words upon the page—
You inspire us.
Forever You have claimed us
and all that is;
upon the farthest horizons,
and within ourselves—
Your Truth will be known.
It sparkles everywhere,
upon the mountains,
within the seas,
within our hearts
as we rest upon our knees
in prayer;
You reveal Your Self—
You shine in the breeze
as it glances off the floor,
and kisses our cheeks,
Your Face
knows Itself
in all of us,
no matter what name
we may call ourselves,
for You are the Revealed,

the Manifest Hiddenness
that enlivens and rejuvenates
every particle of beingness
that proclaims Your Presence
Here.

Az Zahir, The Manifest, *Al Batin*, The Hidden,
Az Zahir al Batin, The Manifest of the Hidden,
Ya Rauf, O Most Kind, *Ya Karim*, O Most Generous and Noble,
Ya Halim, O Most Forbearing and Resilient,
Ya Wadud, O Infinitely Loving One

"I was a Hidden Treasure, and I so loved to be known
that I created the two worlds, seen and Unseen,
in order that My Treasure of Generosity and Loving-kindness
might be known."
[*Hadith Qudsi*]

I call to witness the revolving stars,
the planets that run their course and set,
and the night as it darkly falls, and the morn as it softly breathes:
behold, this is indeed the inspired word of a noble Messenger,
with strength endowed,
secure with Him/Her who in Almightiness is enthroned.
[81:15–20]

It is for those who remain conscious of their Sustainer
that lofty mansions one above another have been built,
and beneath them flow rivers.
The Promise of God;
never does God fail in His/Her Promise.
[39:20]

He/She is the Sustainer of the Worlds.
He/She established the mountains standing high above it

and bestowed blessings on the earth,
and measured all things there to give them nourishment
in due proportion.
[41:9–10]

We will show them Our signs on the farthest horizons and within themselves,
until they know the Truth.
[41:53–54]

Now, indeed, We have conferred dignity upon the children of Adam,
and borne them over land and sea,
and provided for them sustenance out of the good things of life,
and favored them beyond much of Our creation.
[17:70]

The same clear Path has He/She established for you
as that which He/She enjoined on Noah,
that which We have sent by inspiration to you,
and that which We designated for Abraham, Moses, and Jesus:
that you should steadfastly uphold the Faith
and make no divisions within it.
To those who worship other things than God,
the way to which you call them may appear difficult.
God draws to Himself/Herself those who are willing
and guides to Himself/Herself everyone who turns to Him/Her.
[42:13]

He/She has created the heavens and the earth in accordance with Truth
and has shaped you and made your shapes beautiful;
and with Him/Her is your journey's end.
He/She knows what is in the heavens and on earth;
He/She knows what you conceal and what you reveal:
yes, God knows well the secrets of hearts.
[64:3–4]

*Say: "None in the heavens or on earth
knows the hidden reality; no one knows it but God."*
[27:65]

*Limitless in His/Her glory is your Sustainer, the Sustainer of Nobility—
far beyond anything by which they may attempt to define Him/Her!
And peace be with all the Messengers!
And all praise belongs to God alone, the Sustainer of all the Worlds.*
[37:180–182]

77. Al Waali, The Guardian, Bestower of Bounty & 78. Al Muta'ali, The Supremely High

Ya Waali, Ya Muta'ali

We think
we're climbing high
when we mount Everest,
or swing out over cliffs by plane
rising to the clouds.
Yet, level by level, You ascend us
beyond the moon,
the stars,
shining brighter than the sun.
Your Light pours through velvet darkness
alive with the energy of birth—
Ya 'Ali, higher still
in beauty and in power;
Al Muta'ali,
Supremely High, beyond
our telescopes' capacity to see,
and, yet, within
we hold the key
to Your Transcendent Sight.
Riding on a raindrop we can find You,
moving down sidewalks to the Sea;
carried aloft by Your breezes
our hearts can soar
beyond Infinity
into the timeless, spaceless place
of Your Abode,
You who have no shape
yet are the Shaper,
through Your gifts
we can know You
in a moment,

through Your Seeing,
bringing us near,
Ya Muta'ali, Ya 'Alim, Ya Waali.

Ya Waali, O Guardian, Bestower of Bounty,
Ya Muta'ali, O Supremely High,
Ya 'Alim, O All Knowing One

For each there are angels before and behind him/her:
they guard him/her by the command of God.
Truly, God will never change a people's lot
unless they change what is in their hearts.
[13:11]

It is God who has raised the heavens without any supports that you could see,
and is established on the Throne of His/Her Almightiness;
and He/She has made the sun and the moon in service,
each running its course for a determined term. He/She governs all that exists.
Clearly does He/She spell out these messages, so that you might be certain
in your inmost being that you are destined to meet your Sustainer.
And it is He/She who has spread the earth wide
and placed on it firm mountains and running waters.
[13:2–3]

Are you more difficult to create
than the heaven which He/She has constructed?
High has He/She raised its vault and shaped its proportion;
and He/She has made dark its night and brought forth its light of day.
And after that, the earth: wide has He/She spread its expanse,
and has brought its waters out of it, and its pastures,
and has made the mountains firm—
for you and your animals to enjoy.
[79:27–33]

Had We bestowed this Quran from on high upon a mountain,
you would indeed see it humbling itself, breaking asunder in awe of God....
And such parables We offer to human beings, so that they might reflect.
[59:21]

Behold: when the waters burst beyond all limits,
it was We who caused you to be carried in that floating ark,
so that We might make all this a reminder to you all,
and that every wide-awake ear might consciously hear.
[69:11–12]

Do, then, they never gaze at the clouds heavy with water,
how they are created?
And at the sky, how it is raised high?
And at the mountains, how firmly they are settled?
And at the earth, how it is outspread?
[88:17–20]

And God's is the knowledge of the hidden reality
of the heavens and the earth.
And so, the coming of the Hour
will manifest itself like the twinkling of an eye, or nearer still:
for, behold, God has the power to will anything.
And God has brought you forth
from your mothers' wombs knowing nothing—
but He/She has endowed you with hearing,
and sight, and ardent hearts,
so that you might have cause to be grateful.
Have, then, they never considered the birds, enabled to fly in mid-air,
with none but God holding them aloft?
In this, behold, there are messages indeed for people who have faith!
[16:77–79]

It is He/She who displays before you the lightning
to engender both fear and hope;

*It is He/She who raises up the clouds heavy with rain,
and the thunder repeats His/Her praises, and so do the angels
with awe.*
[13:12–13]

"God says, 'I have readied for My righteous servants
what no eye has ever seen,
and no ear has ever heard,
and no heart of a human being has ever conceived.'"
[*Hadith* of the Prophet Muhammad]

79. Al Barr, The Bestower of Beneficence
& 90. Al Mani, The Protector from Harm
& 91. Ad Darr, The Afflicter, The Creator of the Harmful
& 92. An Nafi, The Creator of All Good

Ya Barr, Al Mani, Ad Darr, An Nafi

O Bestower of Beneficence,
again and again,
You have graced us
with Your Favor
and warded off
the scorching winds.
We called upon You
and You have shown us
Kindness and Mercy.
You are our Protector
from all Harm,
the One who withholds
the tides
that would
inundate us
before we have the capacity
to swim,
and the winds that would blow us
off course,
You Who Are All Goodness—
any harm created
must serve blessing,
cracking open
these chests
of Your Goodness
that we might stand
stronger

in Your Light
and learn
the strength
of these muscles
that must contract
in order to serve
and move us forward
in Your Grace—
Ya Nafi,
You Who Are Our Benefactor,
eternally
bringing us
into the Garden
of clear springs,
if of a sudden
all our water
were to vanish
from beneath us
who but our Lord
would provide us
the fresh water that we need,
from clear,
uncontaminated springs?
Subhanallah
Ya Malik ul Mulk,
You know our need
before we voice it.
May the cup we pass
from hand to hand
hold
the water of felicity
that You have graced,
that we might quench each other's thirst
from the springs within Your Garden
even while
we live

here
upon this earth.
With each breath
You resurrect us.
Let us recognize our life
is but Your Living
through us,
Ya Barr,
Ya Mani,
Ya Wadud,
Ya Hayy,
Ya Qayyum,
O Self-Subsisting
Eternal Source of Being!

Ya Barr, O Bestower of Beneficence,
Ya Mani, O Preventer of Harm,
Ad Darr, The Afflicter, The Creator of the Harmful,
An Nafi, The Creator of Good,
Ya Wadud, O Infinitely Loving One,
Ya Hayy, O Ever Living One,
Ya Qayyum, O Self-Subsisting Eternal Source of Being,
Subhanallah Ya Malik ul Mulk, Glory be to You,
O Sovereign of the Complete Dominion

*And so God has graced us with His/Her favor,
and has warded off from us all suffering through the scorching winds.
Truly, we did invoke Him/Her before this:
He/She alone is Truly the Bestower of Beneficence,
Infinitely Merciful!*
[52:27–28]

*Is there any that could provide you with sustenance
if He/She should withhold His/Her provision?*
[67:21]

*If God touches you with affliction, none can remove it but He/She;
if He/She touches you with happiness, He/She has power over all things.*
[6:17]

*And God has given you the capacity to make your houses places of rest,
and has endowed you with dwellings of the skins of animals—
easy for you to handle when you travel and when you camp—
and furnishings and goods for temporary use of their strong wool,
and their soft, furry wool, and their hair.
And among the many objects of His/Her creation,
God has appointed for you sheltering protection:
thus, He/She has given you in the mountains places of repose,
and has endowed you with garments to protect you from heat and cold,
as well as such garments as might protect you from your own violence.
In this way does He/She bestow
the full measure of His/Her blessings on you,
so that you might surrender yourselves unto Him/Her.*
[16:80–81]

In Your Hand is all good.
[3:26]

*God erases all falsehood and by His/Her words proves the truth to be true.
Truly, He/She has full knowledge of what is in hearts;
and it is He/She who accepts repentance from His/Her servants,
and pardons ill deeds, and knows all that you do,
and responds unto all who attain to faith
and do deeds of wholeness and reconciliation.*
[42:24–26]

*All the faithful are but siblings. So, always make peace
between your two siblings, and remain conscious of God,
so that you might be graced with His/Her mercy.*
[49:10]

My Mercy encompasses everything.
[7:156]

Are they, then, not aware that it is God who grants abundant sustenance,
or gives it in scant measure, unto whomever He / She wills?
In this, behold, there are messages indeed for people who will have faith!
And so, give his or her due to the near of kin,
as well as to the needy and the wayfarer;
this is best for all who seek God's Countenance:
for it is they, they that shall attain to a happy state!
[30:37–38]

For they who have attained to faith in God and His / Her Messengers—
it is they, they who uphold the Truth,
and they who bear witness before their Sustainer:
they shall have their reward and their light!
[57:19]

The sincere servants of God,
for them is an appointed nourishment—
fruits, and honor, and dignity,
in gardens of felicity,
facing each other on thrones of happiness:
a cup will be passed around from a clear-flowing fountain,
crystal-clear and delightful to those who drink of it.
[37:40–46]

With goblets shining and cups filled from clear, unsullied springs
by which their minds will not be clouded.
[56:18]

Truly, those who have faith and do deeds of wholeness and reconciliation
their Sustainer will guide by means of their faith:
beneath them will flow rivers in Gardens of Bliss.
There they will call out:
"Glory be to You, O God!"

and they will be answered with the greeting, "Peace!"
And the completion of their cry will be:
"Praise be to God, the Cherisher and Sustainer of all the Worlds!"
[10:9–10]

80. At Tawwab, The One Who Turns Us in Repentance and Accepts Our Repentance

Ya Tawwab, Ya Wajid

O You who turn us into repentance
that we might return to You
with clear hearts,
even as the muddy stream
releases its sediment
before it merges with the sea,
wash clear these hearts
that we might find You,
Ya Wajid.
Even the purest mountain stream
sometimes gathers sticks and straws,
pasture land run-off,
even snakes,
along its course.
Free us of the debris of our traversals
through the neighborhoods of life.
Clear our vision of the murky waters
of misplaced desires,
distractions, and dalliance—
that which holds us captive;
set us free
in Your Remembrance,
Ya Tawwab.
We turn around You
in continual *tawaf*,
circumambulating with the angels,
even as Adam in his regret,
to focus only on Your smile.
Yes, we are forgiven
when we ask it of You.

Yes, You turn us
step by step,
so that again we find
the Way Home,
and in that finding,
rejoice in Being One
again with You, Al Wujud.

Ya Tawwab, O You Who Are Ever Returning,
Acceptor of Repentance,
Ya Wajid, O Finder, You Who Perceive Us
(and grant us being in Your Existence—
the Only One Who Truly Exists, *Al Wujud*—
that we might discover
al Tawhid al Wujud, the "Oneness of Being")

Celebrate your Sustainer's limitless glory,
and praise Him/Her, and seek His/Her forgiveness:
for, behold, He/She is Ever an Acceptor of Repentance.
[110:3]

They came to know with certainty
that there is no refuge from God other than a return to Him/Her;
and so He/She turned again unto them in His/Her mercy,
so that they might repent:
truly, God alone is the Acceptor of Repentance, Infinitely Merciful.
O you who have attained to faith! Remain conscious of God,
and be among those who are true to their word!
[9:118–119]

They who repent and attain to faith and do righteous deeds—
for it is they whose former ill deeds God will transform into good ones—
seeing that God is indeed Oft Forgiving, Infinitely Merciful,
and seeing that he or she who repents

and from then onward does what is right
has truly turned unto God in repentance.
[25:70-71]

Truly, God loves those who turn unto Him/Her in repentance,
and He/She loves those who keep themselves pure.
[2:222]

"O my people, ask your Sustainer to forgive you your mistakes,
and then turn towards Him/Her in repentance—
He/She will shower upon you heavenly blessings in abundance,
and will add strength to your strength."
[11:52, words of the Prophet Hud]

And unto the Thamud We sent their brother Salih.
He said: "O my people! Worship God:
you have no deity other than Him/Her—
He/She brought you into being from the earth,
and made you thrive upon it.
So ask Him/Her to forgive you your mistakes,
and then turn towards Him/Her in repentance—
for, truly, my Sustainer is Ever Near, Ever Responsive!"
[11:61]

81. Al Muntaqim, The Rectifier

Al Muntaqim, Al 'Adl

Swiftly You arrive
to rectify
what we have thrown
off balance.
A potter knows
how quickly the clay
loses its shape
when it flies off center.
There are times Your Justice
must strike swiftly
before more children die
from others' greed
and the leeway
is tangled in a storm
of our own knotting;
when a laborer
sees his work
go up in smoke
from a drunkard's
thoughtless lantern.
Your fire burns clean.
Your swift stringency
rights our course.
The earth cries out for Your help
and for the helpless.
You have shown us
how to treat orphans.
You raised Muhammad high
in Your embrace
and honored his word
with Your guidance.

Cauterize our wounds
and seal our lips,
pour Your honeyed balm,
until we, too, can speak
only Love.

Al Muntaqim, The Rectifier, Avenger of Harm
Al ʿAdl, The Most Just

Step by step He/She has sent down to you this book,
setting forth the truth which confirms
whatever remains of earlier revelations:
for it is He/She who earlier bestowed from on high
the Torah and the Gospel, as a guidance to humankind,
and it is He/She who has bestowed the standard for discernment.
Witness: grievous suffering awaits
those who insist on denying God's signs—
for God is Almighty, the Rectifier of All Harm.
Truly, nothing on earth or in the heavens is hidden from God.
It is He/She who shapes you in the wombs as He/She wills.
There is no deity but Hu, the Almighty, the Truly Wise.
[3:3–6]

Don't despair over things that pass you by
nor exult over blessings that come to you.
For God does not love those who are conceited and boastful,
those who are grasping and encourage others to be greedy.
And as for the one who turns his back—truly, God alone is Self-Sufficient,
the One to Whom All Praise Is Due.
[57:23–24]

Can you, then, [O Muhammad] make the deaf hear,
or show the right way to the blind
or to those who have clearly wandered in error?

But whether We take you away—
truly, We shall bring Our rectification upon them;
or whether We show you the fulfillment of what We have promised them—
truly, We have full power over them!
So hold fast to that which has been revealed to you:
for, truly, you are on a straight way;
and, indeed, this shall become a remembrance for you and your people:
but in time you all will be called to account.
[43:40–44]

The Lord wields righteousness and judgment
for all who are oppressed.
He made known His ways to Moses,
His acts to the children of Israel.
The Lord is Merciful and Gracious,
slow to anger, and plenteous in Mercy.
He will not always chide: neither will He keep His anger forever.
He has not dealt with us after our sin;
nor rewarded us according to our errors.
For as the heaven is high above earth, so great is His Mercy
towards those who are conscious of Him.
As far as the east is from the west,
even so far has He removed our ill deeds from us.
[The Bible, Psalm 103: 6–12]

Strive among yourselves to attain your Sustainer's forgiveness
and a paradise as vast as the heavens and the earth,
which has been readied for those who are conscious of God—
who spend in His way in times of abundance and in times of hardship,
and hold in check their anger, and pardon their fellow human beings,
because God loves those who do good;
and who, when they have committed a shameful deed
or have otherwise wronged their own souls,
remember God
and pray for forgiveness for their mistakes—
for who can forgive sins but God?—

*and do not knowingly persist
in doing whatever wrong they may have done.*
[3:133–135]

*O you who have faith!
Be conscious of God with all the consciousness that is due Him/Her,
and do not allow death to overtake you
before you have surrendered yourselves to Him/Her.
And hold fast, all together, to the rope of God,
and do not draw apart from one another.
And remember with gratitude the blessings which God has bestowed on you:
how, when you were adversaries, He/She brought your hearts together,
so that through His/Her blessings you became as though of one family;
and how when you were on the brink of a fiery abyss,
He/She saved you from it.
In this way, God makes clear His/Her signs to you,
so that you might be guided,
and that there might grow out of you a community
who invite to all that is good, and who encourage the doing of what is right
and forbid the doing of what is wrong:
and it is they who shall attain happiness!*
[3:102–4]

83. Ar Rauf, The Most Kind

Ya Rauf, Ya Samad, Ya Rahim, Ya Salaam

"Be kind,
unwind
the tangles
of the heart
of those who come
near to your influential sphere,
and beyond—
wherever you see pain,
bring the balm
of compassion."
We know
what it is to be troubled,
to bear concern
for children,
for livelihood,
for love;
can we not
stretch ourselves,
our hands,
our hearts
to soothe
where it is needed?
Ya Rauf,
continually
You extend
Your Love
through us,
when we awaken
to a heart crying out in need,
a heart that may not yet even know
the seed of its pain,

and yet may crack open
through Your Grace
and discover its flourishing—
You give us so many ways
to grow,
to find again
the Source of our Sustenance—
let us remember
that we are all dying,
to be born anew
in Your Radiance,
Ya Nur,
Ya Rahman,
Ya Rahim.
Let us be
Your Hand of Mercy,
a midwife of Your Love,
welcoming
each of Your dear children
into the Greenness
of Your Garden of Peace,
for we are all the offspring
of Your Love and Your Generosity,
longing to be known.
O You Who Are Eternally Kind,
let us bless each other's hearts
with the Peace of Your Compassion.
Ya Wadud,
Ya Karim,
Ya Rauf,
Ya Salaam.

> *Ya Rauf*, O You Who Are Infinitely and Eternally Kind,
> *Ya Samad*, O Eternal Satisfier of All Need,
> *Ya Rahim*, O Infinitely Merciful One,
> *Ya Nur*, O You Who Are Light,

Ya Rahman, O Infinitely Compassionate One,
Ya Wadud, O Infinitely Loving One,
Ya Karim, O Infinitely Generous One,
Ya Salaam, O You Who Are Peace

*It is God who sends to His/Her servants clear signs
that He/She may lead you out of the depths of darkness into the Light.
And truly, God is to you Infinitely Kind and Infinitely Merciful.*
[57:9]

*O humankind! there has come to you a direction from your Lord
and a healing for your hearts
and for those who have faith, guidance and grace.
Say: "In the abundance of God and in His grace,
in that let them rejoice;
that is better than whatever they may hoard."*
[10:57–58]

*Say: "Truly, my Instructor has guided me
onto a straight way through a steadfast faith—
the way of Abraham, the true one,
who was not of those who attribute divinity to anything beside God."
Say: "Truly, my prayer, and all my acts of worship,
and my living and my dying are for God alone,
the Sustainer of all worlds."*
[6:161–162]

*It is He/She who has made you His/Her representatives on earth:
He/She has raised you in ranks, some above others,
that He/She may test you with the gifts He/She has given
for your Sustainer is swift with stringency,
yet Ever Ready to Forgive, Infinitely Merciful.*
[6:165]

*Say: "Whether you conceal what is in your hearts
or bring it into the open, God knows it:*

*for He/She knows all that is in the heavens and all that is on earth;
and God has the power to will anything."
On the Day when every human being will find himself or herself
faced with all the good that he or she has done,
and with all the harm that he or she has done,
there are those who will wish
that there were a long span of time between themselves and that Day.
And so, God counsels you to be conscious of Him/Her;
God is Eternally Kind towards His/Her creatures.*
[3:29–30]

*Those who love all that come to them in search of refuge,
and who harbor in their hearts no grudge
for whatever the others may have been given,
but rather give them preference over themselves,
even though poverty may be their own lot:
for such as from their own covetousness are saved—
it is they, they that shall attain to a happy state!
And so, they who come after them pray:
"O our Sustainer! Forgive us our sin, our errors,
as well as those of our brothers and sisters who preceded us in faith,
and let not our hearts entertain any unworthy thoughts or feelings
against any of those who have faith.
O our Sustainer!
Truly, You are Eternally Kind, Infinitely Merciful!"*
[59:9–10]

God invites to the Abode of Peace.
[10:25]

84. Al Malik ul Mulk, The Sovereign of the Dominion

Ya Malik al Mulk

Morning has come
and we jump online
to hear the Word
of the day.
Always You keep posting
the good news
of Your welcome
to hearts who have gone astray
and strangers who are searching
for a place to lay their heads,
through the open hearts
of servants of Your Love.
You have spread out before us
a gracious land,
spacious in its lying down
and in its rising up.
This earth belongs to You,
and the starlit heavens.
How could we pretend to own it,
when we would have so few ideas
as to how to recreate it?
We glimpse a portion of its miracle
and then begin to recognize
how much greater
than ever we imagined
is even the functioning
within a single cell.
All the species,
that hold the secrets of our healing,
hover near,
waiting in the balance.

We must awaken
to care for Your Creation
while there is still time
in the glass of our desire.
We never know when the moment
will arrive when You will call
to bring us Home.
May we be good trustees
of the palms and oaks
and of each other's hearts.
Water spills from the fountain
and all Your birds come to drink—
it is not yours or mine,
but Yours,
O Owner of the Kingdom,
Ya Malik al Mulk!

Ya Malik al Mulk, O Sovereign of the Kingdom

A Divine writ—
with messages that have been made clear in and by themselves,
and have been distinctly spelled out as well—
out of the grace of One who is All Wise, All Aware,
so that you may worship none but God—
"Behold, I come unto you from Him/Her
as a warner and a bearer of glad tidings."
[11:1-2]

For to God belong the forces of the heavens and the earth;
and God is Almighty, All Wise.
We have truly sent you as a witness, as a bringer of joyful news,
and as a warner: so that you, O people,
may have faith in God and His/Her Messenger,

that you might assist and honor God
and celebrate His/Her praises morning and evening.
[48:7–9]

And to God belongs the dominion over the heavens and the earth;
and God has power over all things.
Truly, in the creation of the heavens and the earth,
and in the succession of night and day,
there are indeed signs for all who are endowed with insight,
and who remember God standing, and sitting,
and when they lie down to sleep,
and contemplate creation—of the heavens and the earth:
"O our Sustainer! You have not created this without meaning and purpose.
Limitless are You in Your subtle glory!"
[3:189–91]

Don't you see how God has created the seven heavens in harmony
and made the moon a light in their midst
and made the sun a glorious lamp?
And how God has caused you to grow gradually from the earth,
and in the end He will return you to it
and then raise you forth anew?
And God has unfolded wide the earth for you
that you might move about there on spacious paths.
[71:15–20]

God bestows His dominion upon whom He wills:
for God is Infinite, All Knowing.
And their prophet said to them:
"Behold, it shall be a sign of his rightful dominion
that you will be granted a heart
endowed by your Sustainer with inner peace and with all that is enduring
in the angel-borne heritage
left behind by the House of Moses and the House of Aaron.
Herein, behold, there shall indeed be a sign for you if you are of the faithful."
[2:247–8]

Call to your Sustainer humbly, and in the secrecy of your hearts.
Truly, He/She does not love those who go beyond the bounds
of what is right.
And so, do not spread corruption on earth
after it has been so well ordered.
And call to Him/Her with awe and longing:
truly, God's grace is very near those who do good.
And He/She it is who sends the winds
as joyous news of His coming grace—
so that, when they have brought heavy clouds
We may drive them towards dead land and cause rain to descend;
that by it We may cause all manner of fruitfulness to spring forth.
Even so shall We cause the dead to emerge—
perhaps you will remember.
[7:55–57]

Don't they look at the sky above them?
How We have made it and adorned it
and how there are no flaws in it?
And the earth—We have spread it wide
and firmly established mountains on it
and caused it to bring forth every kind of beautiful growth,
so offering an insight and a reminder
to every human being who willingly turns to God.
And We send down from the sky rain charged with blessing
and with it cause gardens to grow, and fields of grain,
and tall palm-trees with their thickly-clustered dates,
as sustenance for human beings;
and by all this We bring dead land to life:
even so will be the Resurrection.
[50:6–11]

To God belongs all that is in the heavens and all that is on earth;
and all things are returning to God.
[3:109]

85. Zhul Jalali wal Ikram, Lord of Power and Abundant Beneficence

Ya Zhul Jalali wal Ikram, Ya Wadud, Ya Rahman, Ya Rahim

O Lord of Power
and Abundant Beneficence,
You have so much to teach us,
and we are watching,
waiting upon Your Word,
to witness all the beauties
You keep pouring
and to learn—
such Magnificence and Honor,
Ya Zhul Jalali wal Ikram,
You who endow with such generosity
we cannot even describe
the extent
of Your Beauty and Your Wisdom
with which You shower us,
with praise of You that purifies.
Your Name upon our lips
unlocks the treasure of Your Being
that is everywhere apparent,
so much that sometimes it is hidden—
within the ruins of our hearts
when we have broken open,
because there was no way to encompass
You within our limits,
O Most Magnificent Power
of Being, of Love,
in love we begin to see
all the Beauty
You would have us know,
and any ugliness melts away,

because it is simply a lack
of our perception and our action,
and You are all pervading,
ready to arrive,
in our awareness,
through all our movement,
whenever we open our eyes,
and turn to become
that which You would have us be,
O Source of Infinite Compassion,
and Infinite Mercy.

Ya Zhul Jalali wal Ikram, O Lord of Majestic Power
and Abundant Beneficence,
Lord of Majesty, Bounty, and Honor,
Ya Wadud, O Infinitely Loving One
Ya Rahman, O Infinitely Compassionate,
Ya Rahim, O Infinitely Merciful One

All that is in the heavens and all that is on earth
acclaims the limitless glory of God,
the Supreme Sovereign, the Holy, the Almighty, the All Wise!
He/She it is who has sent unto the unlettered people
a Messenger from among themselves,
to convey unto them His/Her Signs, and to cause them to grow in purity,
and to impart to them revelation as well as wisdom.
[62:1–2]

Behold, as for those who say, "Our Sustainer is God,"
and then steadfastly pursue the right way—angels often come down to them:
"Do not fear and do not grieve, but receive the glad news of the Garden
which you were promised!
We are your protectors in the life of this world and in the Hereafter.
There you shall have all that for which your souls long;
there you shall have all that you ask for!

A welcoming gift from One Oft Forgiving, Most Merciful!"
And who could be better of speech than one who invites people to God,
and does what is just and right, and says,
"Truly, I am of those who surrender themselves to God"?
Good and evil cannot be equal, so repel evil
with that which is more beautiful—
and lo! he or she between whom and yourself was enmity
may become as though they had always been a close, true friend!
Yet this is not given to any but those who are patient in adversity;
it is not given to any but those endowed with the mightiest of good fortune!
[41:30–35]

Reclining upon meadows green and rich carpets of beauty—
which, then, of the favors of your Lord will you deny?
Blessed be the Name of your Lord,
the Lord of Power and Abundant Beneficence!
[55:76–78]

As for man, his days are as grass:
as a flower of the field, so he flourishes.
For the wind passes over it, and it is gone:
and the place thereof shall know it no more.
But the Mercy of the Lord is from Everlasting to Everlasting,
upon those who are conscious of Him,
and His righteousness unto children's children,
to such as keep their bond with Him,
and to those who so remember His commandments as to do them.
The Lord has prepared His Throne in the heavens;
and His kingdom rules over all.
Bless the Lord, O you, his angels, that excel in strength,
that do His commandments, hearkening unto the voice of His word.
Bless the Lord, all of you, his hosts;
O you ministers of His, that do His pleasure.
Bless the Lord, all His works in all places of His dominion:
bless the Lord, O my soul.
[The Bible, Psalm 103: 15–22]

*All that is on earth or in the heavens is bound to pass away,
but forever will abide the Face of your Lord,
Full of Majesty, Bounty, and Honor.
Which, then, of your Lord's blessings will you deny?*
[55:26–28]

Remember Me; I remember you.
[2:152]

86. Al Muqsit, The One Who Keeps the Balance, the Equitable

Al Muqsit, Al Mumin, Al Haqq

You hold the keys.
Too often we run,
on autopilot,
and forget to see
if You have turned the key
in the lock.
Suddenly, we find ourselves out on a limb,
falling, for lack of support
from the trunk
we have forgotten,
as we clamber
out into space
reaching
for our desires.
You give us space to choose,
and yet You choose
to keep the balance
of our hearts close to You,
Alhamdulillah!
It is not gold in sacks
You care for from these limbs,
but a heart that is golden
in Your Light.
Where do we carry You
in our flight?
Your angels
bring us Home,
sometimes when
we least expect it.
Let us rectify our own accounts,

keeping faith
with the word
we have given,
"Yes."
We would not be here
if we did not have the capacity
to try—
in Your Eye,
all may be forgiven
if we turn
with a heart full of longing
for Truth.

Al Muqsit, The One Who Keeps the Balance, The Equitable,
Al Mumin, The Most Faithful, Inspirer of Faith, *Al Haqq*, The Truth

God offers signs—and so do the angels
and all who are endowed with knowledge—
that there is no god except God, the Keeper of the Balance:
there is no deity but Hu, the Almighty, the Truly Wise.
[3:18]

For with God are the keys to the Unseen:
the treasures that none knows but He/She.
And He/She knows all that is on the land and in the sea;
and not a leaf falls but He/She knows it;
and neither is there a seed in the earth's deep darkness,
nor anything alive or dead, but is recorded in a clear record.
And He/She it is who causes you to be as dead at night,
and knows what you do during the day;
and each day He/She brings you back to life
so that a term set by Him/Her might be fulfilled.
In the end, to Him/Her you must return;
and He/She will make you understand all that you did.
[6:59–60]

Say: "O my Servants who have transgressed against your own selves!
Do not despair of Allah's Compassion:
for Allah forgives all mistakes:
for He/She is Oft Forgiving, Infinitely Merciful.
Turn to your Sustainer and surrender to Him/Her
before the suffering comes upon you—
since after that you will not be helped—
before the consequence suddenly
comes upon you without your perceiving it,
follow the best of that which your Sustainer has revealed to you!"
[39:53–55]

O you who have attained to faith!
Do not deprive yourselves of the good things of life
which God has made lawful to you,
but do not transgress the bounds of what is right:
truly, God does not love those who go beyond the bounds of what is right.
And so partake of the lawful, good things which God grants you as sustenance,
and be conscious of God, in whom you have faith.
[5:87–88]

And He/She alone holds sway over His/Her servants.
And He/She sends forth heavenly guardians to watch over you
until, when death approaches any of you,
Our messengers cause him or her to die:
and not one do they overlook.
And those are then returned before God,
the Protector Who Truly Brings Near.
Oh, truly, judgment is His/Hers alone,
and He/She is the swiftest of reckoners.
[6:61–62]

Does God not know best those who are grateful to Him/Her?
And when those who have faith in our signs come to you,
say: "Peace be with you.
Your Sustainer has willed upon Himself/Herself

the law of compassion—
so that if any of you does harm out of ignorance,
and afterwards repents and changes,
Your Sustainer is Ever Ready to Forgive, Most Merciful."
[6:53–54]

And everything, be it small or great, is recorded.
Behold, the God-conscious will find themselves
in gardens with flowing waters,
in a seat of Truth,
in the Presence of a Sovereign who determines all things.
[54:53–55]

87. Al Jami, The Gatherer

Ya Jami, Ya Wadud

Ya Jami,
You reunite
the disparate;
when we fall
away from our center,
You bring us back
to wholeness.
You reassemble us
in ranks of strength,
for standing together
we are strong in Your Love.
It is You who feed us.
Families, associations,
may we remember
that there are no limits
to Your Loving,
that from hand to hand
we are interwoven
by less than six degrees,
east to west
and north to south,
in this grand basket of Being
that holds life
everywhere
among us,
this web, that vibrates
with the breeze
of Your Love,
and wraps around our world,
angels on our shoulders
up to the Throne,

circle upon circle,
singing chants of Your remembrance,
and in that remembrance
we are reborn,
recollected,
in You,
Ya Jami, Ya Wadud.

> *Ya Jami*, O You Who Gather,
> *Ya Wadud*, O Infinitely Loving One

> *"O our Sustainer! Truly, You will gather humankind together*
> *to witness the Day about which there is no doubt:*
> *truly, God never fails to fulfill His/Her promise."*
> [3:9]

> *God will bring us all together, and with Him/Her is all journeys' end.*
> [42:15]

> *Recite what is sent of the Book by inspiration to you*
> *and establish regular prayer:*
> *for prayer restrains from shameful and unjust deeds,*
> *and remembrance (zhikr) of God is surely the greatest of all.*
> *And God knows that which you do.*
> [29:45]

> *In the case of those who say, "Our Lord is Allah,"*
> *and, further, stand straight and steadfast,*
> *the angels descend upon them: "Fear not! Nor grieve!*
> *But receive the Glad Tidings of the Garden,*
> *that which you were promised!"*
> [41:30]

> *By those who range themselves in ranks*
> *and so are strong in repelling harm,*

and so proclaim the message: Truly, truly, your God is One!
The Sustainer of the heavens and of the earth
and all that is between them,
and Lord of every point of sunrise!
[37:1–5]

O you who have faith! celebrate God's praises, and do this often;
and glorify Him/Her morning and evening.
He/She it is who sends blessings on you as do His/Her angels
that He/She may bring you out of the depths of darkness
into the Light:
and He/She is Full of Mercy to the faithful.
[33:41–43]

"Whenever people sit to remember God, angels cover them
(spreading their wings over them),
and Divine Mercy envelops them;
inner peace descends upon them,
and God mentions them to those who are with Him."
[*Hadith* of the Prophet Muhammad]

The Lord is my shepherd, I shall not want.
He makes me lie down in green pastures,
He leads me beside tranquil waters,
He refreshes my soul.
He guides me along the paths of righteousness for His name's sake.
Even though I walk through the darkest valley,
I will fear no harm, for You are with me;
Your rod and Your staff, they comfort me.
You prepare a table before me in the presence of those who challenge me.
You anoint my head with oil; my cup overflows.
Surely, Your goodness and love will follow me all the days of my life,
and I will dwell in the house of the Lord forever.
[The Bible: Psalm 23 of the Prophet David]

88. Al Ghani, The One Who Is Rich
& 89. Al Mughni, The Enricher

Ya Ghani, Ya Mughni, Ya Basir, Ya Sami, Ya Wadud

Each seed
knows
its own name.
Embedded
in the DNA
is its whole history
of loving—
who is matched
with whom,
and who descended—
in cascading
realms of servanthood
of the One
through whom we are all related,
manifesting the riches
by which we grow—
which are our birthright
as seeds of Your Being,
Ya Ghani, Ya Mughni,
O You Who Are Rich,
and Enrich us all!
Along the way, we unfold
with blue eyes, gray,
green, or brown, and yet
the capacity to see is always Yours.
And even one born blind
knows by heart
the sound of Your Voice
and can recognize
the kindred of the Soul

by the vibrancy
that awakens the skin
even of the deaf.
Yes, turn and turn again;
spiraling
through the language
of our Source.
We dance in Your air
loved by Love Itself.
Ya Basir, Ya Sami, Ya Wadud.

Ya Ghani, O You Who Are Rich,
Ya Mughni, O Enricher of Us All,
Ya Basir, O You Who Are All Seeing,
Ya Sami, O You Who Are All Hearing,
Ya Wadud, O Infinitely Loving One!

Do you see the seed that you sow in the ground?
Is it you that causes it to grow or are We the cause?
[56:63–64]

It is He/She who has created you all out of one soul,
and out of it brought into being a mate,
so that man might incline with love towards woman.
And so, when he has embraced her, she conceives a light burden,
and continues to bear it.
Then, when she grows heavy, they both pray to God, their Sustainer:
"If You grant us a righteous child,
we shall most certainly be among the grateful."
[7:189]

O you who have faith!
Spend on others out of the good things which you may have acquired,
and out of that which We bring forth for you out of the earth;
and do not choose for your spending

anything bad which you yourselves would not accept
without averting your eyes in disdain.
And know that God is the One Who is Rich,
the One Worthy of Praise.
[2:267]

So recite then as much of the Quran as may be easy;
and be constant in prayer and spend in charity;
and loan to God a beautiful loan.
And whatever good you send forth for your souls,
you shall find it in God's Presence richer and better in reward.
And always seek God's grace:
for God is Ever Ready to Forgive, Most Merciful.
[73:20]

God has revealed the most beautiful message
in the form of a Book consistent within itself,
repeating its teaching in various guises—
the skins of those who stand in awe of their Lord tremble with it;
then their skins and their hearts soften with the remembrance of God.
Such is God's guidance:
with it He/She guides the one who wills to be guided.
[39:23]

God is Infinite, All Knowing, granting wisdom to whom He/She wills:
and whoever is granted wisdom
has indeed been granted abundant wealth,
but none bears this in mind except those who are gifted with insight.
[2:268–9]

Behold, it is you who are called upon to spend freely in God's cause:
but among you are such as turn out to be stingy!
And yet, he or she who is stingy is but stingy towards his or her own self:
for God is indeed the One Who Is Rich, Self-Sufficient,
while it is you who are in need.
[47:38]

*Say: "God has spoken the truth:
follow, then, the creed of Abraham,
who turned away from all that is false,
and was not of those who ascribe divinity to anything beside God."
Behold, the first Temple ever set up for humankind
was indeed the one at Bakkah:[33]
rich in blessing, and a guidance to all the worlds, full of clear messages—
the place where Abraham once stood; and whoever enters it finds inner peace.
And so, pilgrimage to the Temple is a responsibility, and belongs to God,
for all people who are able to undertake it.
And as for those who turn away from the truth—
truly, God is the One Who Is Rich Without Need.*
[3:95–97]

*Truly, those who have faith and do righteous deeds
the Infinitely Compassionate will endow with love.*
[19:96]

---

33 "Bakkah" is understood as Mecca (Makkah). In some older Arabic dialects, the consonants *b* and *m* are interchangeable. The Temple in Mecca—that is, the Kaaba—indicates the direction of prayer (*qiblah*) specified in the Quran. The Kaaba was first built by Abraham and Ishmael, before the Temple of Solomon in Jerusalem; in turning towards the Kaaba, we follow Abraham's example and turn towards the inner heart where we are closest to our Sustainer, and find peace, for *God invites to the abode of peace.* [10:25]

93. An Nur, The Light

Ya Nur, Ya Wasi, Ya Wadud

And today,
Your Light returns,
bouncing from Your leaves
to my heart
through the window that opens
to Your Vastness.
From where I sit,
I cannot quite see
Your sun rise,
yet through the mirror,
a hidden window opens,
and Your rose
pours through
the air, reverberating
with Your silent Song of Love.
It is everywhere,
washing us from head to toe
and beyond our arm's expanse,
evening out the ripples
of missed beats
of our hearts.
The ocean of Your Love
surges
every day and night—
when we have forgotten
to listen
or to look
for Your Sweet Presence,
still,
we rest in Your arms,
All the while, God encompasses them,

without their even being aware of it.
As we are reminded
by Your constellations
shining,
magnifying Your Glory
for all to see
who keep watch
in the night,
woven in such lustrous patterns,
in realms far beyond
the sight of our eyes,
but known by heart—
these hearts
that catch Your silent whispers
and awaken
once again
at dawn—
with the rising of the stars,
with the rising of the moon,
and with the rising of the sun;
"Wake up and see Me."
We bow
before the Beauty
of Your Light
rising in the heart,
Your Light that shines eternally
and melts
whatever may remain
of that which we might
call "self,"
until we are poured
out again, transfigured
in Your Love,
surging
breath by breath.
Ya Nur,

Ya Nur ala Nur,
Subhanallah
Ya Rabb al Alameen,
Ya Wasi, Ya Wadud.

Ya Nur, O You Who Are Light!
Ya Nur ala Nur, Light Upon Light!
Subhanallah, Glory be to God,
Ya Rabb al Alameen, Sustainer of All Worlds!
Ya Wasi, O All Encompassing One,
Ya Wadud, O Infinitely Loving One

God is the Light of the heavens and the earth.
The parable of His/Her light is,
as it were, that of a niche containing a lamp;
the lamp is enclosed in glass, the glass like a radiant star;
lit from a blessed tree—an olive-tree
that is neither of the east nor of the west—
the oil of which would almost give light
even though fire had not touched it: light upon light!
God guides to His/Her light the one who wills to be guided;
and God offers parables to human beings,
since God has full knowledge of all things.
[24:35]

God is the Protector of those who have faith,
leading them out of the depths of darkness into the light.
[2:257]

All the while, God encompasses them,
without their even being aware of it.
[85:20]

He/She is the One who causes the dawn to break;
and He/She has made the night to be a source of stillness,

*and the sun and the moon for reckoning
by the order of the Almighty, the All Knowing.
And He/She it is who has made the stars for you
so that you might be guided by them
through the darknesses of land and sea:
clearly have We detailed Our signs for people of inner knowing.*
[6:96–97]

*And so We gave Abraham insight
into the Mighty Dominion over the heavens and the earth,
so that he might become one of those who are inwardly sure.
Then, when the night overshadowed him with its darkness, he beheld a star.
He exclaimed, "This is my Sustainer!"
But when it set, he said, "I love not that which sets."
Then, when he beheld the moon rising, he said, "This is my Sustainer!"
But when it set, he said, "Indeed, if my Sustainer does not guide me,
I will most certainly become one of the people who go astray!"
Then, when he beheld the sun rising, he said,
"This is my Sustainer! This one is the greatest!"
But when it also set, he exclaimed: "O my people!
Behold, far be it from me to ascribe divinity, as do you,
to anything beside God!
Behold, unto Him/Her who brought into being the heavens and the earth
I have turned my face, having turned away from all that is false."*
[6:75–79]

*Holy is He/She who has set up in the skies great constellations,
and has placed among them a radiant lamp and a moon giving light.
And He/She it is who made the night and the day to follow each other,
for such as have the will to celebrate His/Her praises,
or to show their gratitude.*
[25:61–62]

*One Day you will see the faithful men and the faithful women,
how their Light runs forward before them and to their right:*

"Good news for you today: gardens beneath which running waters flow, where you may live—this, this is the highest achievement!"
[57:12]

Bow down in adoration and draw near!
[96:19]

94. Al Hadi, The Guide

Ya Hadi, Ya Wali

The End and the Beginning belong to You;
the middle is ours to open
as we choose.
Continually You provide signs
and guidance
through the stars and the breezes,
the trees and the vines,
the springs and rivers,
and the intimations of our hearts,
that can recognize the true from the false
if we pay attention.
When we don't,
our way constricts.
Do not say of anything,
"I'll be sure to do it tomorrow,"
without adding, "If God wills!"
And call your Sustainer to mind
when you forget, and say:
"I hope that my Lord will guide me
ever closer even than this to the right path."
When we choose the path
of the generous,
the more our way
is eased towards bliss.
O You Who Respond,
always You are watching to show us the way,
as we feel the brush
of Your Breeze on our cheek,
even in the depths of doubt or despair,
You are with us, wherever we may be.
In stages You lead us

to the pools of righteousness
alive with the fish of Your meaning.[34]
And glories shine in our eyes
from Your Friendship.
As above,
so below;
there is nowhere You are not,
and the vibration keeps attuning us
from the pulse of the earth
to the song of the skies.
May we choose our time,
our companions with care,
softly singing back to You
Your song in our hearts.
Step by step,
we return
with gladness.
Ya Hadi,
Ya Haqq al Wadud.

Ya Hadi, O Guide,
Ya Wali, O Friend and Protector,
Ya Haqq al Wadud, O Truth of Infinite Love

Do not say of anything, "I shall be sure to do so and so tomorrow,"
without adding: "If God wills!"
And call your Sustainer to mind when you forget,

---

[34] The pool of Abraham, near the cave where it is related that he was born, is alive with fish, golden in the morning light. It is said that when Nimrod attempted to fling him into the fire, the fire became cool and turned to water, and the burning embers became bright fish. The fish living there now, adjacent to the mosque, in Sanliurfa, Turkey, are said to be their blessed descendents. Abraham is referred to in the Quran as the "Friend of God" (*Khalil Allah*).

*and say: "I hope that my Lord will guide me
ever closer even than this to the right path."*
[18:23–24]

*None can guide and give support as your Sustainer does!
Now they who insist on denying the truth tend to ask,
"Why hasn't the Quran been bestowed on him from on high
in one single revelation?"
It is so that by this We may strengthen your heart;
and We have related it to you in well-arranged stages,
little by little.*
[25:31–32]

*By the Book that makes things clear—
We sent it down during a blessed night:
for We wish to give counsel.
In wisdom, that night the distinction between all things is clarified,
by command from Our Presence.
For We always are sending guidance
as a mercy from your Sustainer:
for He/She alone is All Hearing, All Seeing;
the Sustainer of the heavens and the earth
and all between them, if only you have inner certainty.*
[44:2–7]

*Say: "Truly, God's guidance is the only guidance:
and so we have been called to surrender ourselves
to the Sustainer of all the worlds,
and to be constant in prayer and conscious of Him/Her:
for it is to Him/Her that we shall all be gathered."*
[6:71–72]

*And whomever God wills to guide, his/her bosom He/She opens wide
with willingness towards self-surrender...
Clearly, indeed, have We spelled out these messages
for people who take them to heart!*

*Theirs shall be an abode of peace with their Sustainer;
and He/She shall be near to them because of what they have been doing.*
[6:125–127]

*And God endows with an ever-deeper consciousness of the right way
those who seek guidance;
and good deeds, the fruits of which endure forever,
are best in the sight of your Sustainer
and yield the best return.*
[19:76]

*So the one who gives and stands in awe of God
and sincerely affirms that which is best,
We will indeed ease for him/her the path to bliss.*
[92:5–7]

*Say: "Holy inspiration has brought it down from your Sustainer in stages,
setting forth the truth, so that it might give firmness
unto those who have attained to faith,
and provide guidance and a glad tiding
unto all who have surrendered themselves to God."*
[16:102]

95. Al Badi, The Skilful Creator, Originator

Ya Badi, Ya Qawi, Ya Rahman

You spoke
and we became.
Will You help us tame
these desires
You implanted in us?
You know our limitations
and our skill;
everything originates with You.
So show us the purpose of these faults we find
that break our concentration in Your Love.
So much to learn,
we find our way only with Your help,
You who imagine all the intricacies
of Compassion
that might fill our hearts.
Seeing someone struggle
reminds us of our own.
We are nothing
without Your Brilliance
that shines through
all the cracks
in our armor;
amour is essential,
not these defenses
we employ
to shield ourselves
from Your expansion and contraction—
even sheets of ice
dissolve
when Your spring arrives,
and cherry blossoms

burst in the orchard,
and we are overwhelmed
with the flood of Your Beauty,
Ya Badi,
Ya Wahhab,
Ya Wadud.

Ya Badi, O Skilful Creator, Originator,
Ya Qawi, The Source of All Power,
Ya Rahman, O Infinitely Compassionate One,
Ya Wahhab, O You Who Overcome Us with Your Infinite Giving,
Ya Wadud, O Infinitely Loving One

The Skilful Originator is He/She of the heavens and the earth:
and when He/She wills a thing to be,
He/She but says to it, "Be" —and it is . . .
Indeed, We have made all the signs manifest
to people who are endowed with inner certainty.
[2:117–118]

Limitless is He/She in His/Her glory,
and sublimely exalted above anything
that people may devise by way of definition:
the Originator of the heavens and the earth!
[6:100–1]

Say: "Travel through the earth
and see how God originated creation.
Even so will God create again,
for God has power over all things."
[29:20]

Their brother Salih said unto them: "Will you not be conscious of God?
Behold, I am a messenger to you, worthy of your trust:
be, then, conscious of God, and pay heed to me!

And no reward whatever do I ask of you for it:
my reward rests with none but the Sustainer of all the worlds.
Do you think that you will be left secure
in the midst of what you have here and now? —
amidst gardens and springs and fields,
and these palm-trees with slender spathes? —
and that you will continue to be able to carve dwellings
out of the mountains with great skill?
Be, then, conscious of God, and pay attention to me,
and pay no mind to the counsel of those who are given to excess—
those who spread corruption on earth, instead of setting things right!"
[26:142–152]

Who is it that has created the heavens and the earth,
and sends down for you water from the skies?
For it is by this means that We cause gardens of shining beauty to grow—
it is not in your power to cause its trees to grow!
Could there be any divine power besides God?
[27:60]

O children of Adam!
Indeed, We have given you garments to cover your nakedness,
and as a thing of beauty;
but the garment of God-consciousness is best of all.
This is one of God's messages—
that human beings might take it to heart.
[7:26]

96. Al Baqi, The Truly Abiding One

Ya Baqi, Ya Karim, Ya Salaam

"*Partake of the good things
We have given you,*
don't transgress
the bounds of consideration
for another's path."
Remember how you,
too, prefer consideration.
One alone remains,
abiding in our hearts
when all else is lost to age
or accident.
Who will answer,
if that One
has not arrived in residence?
Your heart knows the cost
of forgetfulness.
Don't steal another's glances,
another's portion of this earth,
a wife,
a husband,
a home,
a place in Heaven.
Children suffer such
transgressions
and alarm their bones
into fractured existences
that are hard to heal.
You abide
and pour the only salve
that soothes these pains
of restriction.

That which is with You
is best.
May we extend Your Hand through ours
and suffer not the least to fend
for themselves;
may we adorn our lives
with the Most Beautiful remembrance
of You, who have no end to Your Beneficence,
for You are Ever Abiding,
the Only One,
who hears all our prayers
and returns us
all to Peace.

Ya Baqi, O Truly Abiding One,
Ya Karim, O Infinitely Generous One,
Ya Salaam, O You Who Are Peace

Partake of the good things
which We have provided for you as sustenance,
but in doing so, do not transgress the bounds of equity.
Even so, witness, I forgive all sins unto anyone who repents
and attains to faith and does the deeds of wholeness and reconciliation,
and thereafter keeps to the rightful path.
[20:81–82]

Tell the men of faith to lower their gaze
and to be mindful of their chastity:
this will help to increase their purity—
truly, God is aware of all that they do.
And tell the women of faith to lower their gaze
and to be mindful of their chastity.
[24:30–31]

So do not barter away your bond with God for a trifling gain!
Truly, that which is with God is by far the best for you, if only you knew:
what is with you is bound to come to an end,
but that which is with God will endure.
And most certainly shall We grant unto those who are patient in adversity
their reward in accordance with the best of their actions.
[16: 95–96]

Those who have faith and do righteous deeds
will be brought into gardens beneath which running waters flow,
there to dwell by their Sustainer's consent,
and will be welcomed with the greeting, "Peace!"
Are you not aware how God offers the parable of a good word?
It is like a good tree, firmly rooted,
reaching its branches towards the sky,
always yielding fruit, by consent of its Sustainer.
This is how God offers parables to human beings,
so that they might consider the truth.
[14:23–25]

Those who pray: "O our Sustainer!
Grant that our spouses and our offspring may be a joy to our eyes,
and cause us to be foremost among those who are conscious of You!"
These will be rewarded for all their patient perseverance with a high station;
there they shall be met with greetings of welcome and peace,
there to abide—what a beautiful abode and place of rest!
[25:74–76]

For God is the Most Beautiful,
and the One who is Truly Abiding.
[20:73]

97. Al Warith, The Inheritor of All

Ya Warith, Al Khaliq, Al Bari, Al Musawwir, Ya Muhaymin

Oh thank you,
for the gift
of the stars
this morning—
even through
the slats of the blinds,
of this window,
we can see,
and rejoice
to have our sight
lifted
beyond the realms
of pain
of the bodily
existence.
You created us
from motes of light
washed with Your water—
and the Seas
of Being
surged
with Your waves
of Grace
throughout
this fertile land.
Rivers,
streams
of vibrancy
race throughout
this form
to know You,

Al Khaliq,
Al Bari,
Al Musawwir.
And all the
constellations
trace
Your patterns
in the sky
lacing light
throughout the heavens
to engage
these eyes
to know
the Greater,
to uplift these hearts
when we become too weighted
with our daily concerns.
The night
You give us,
in which to rest,
embraced
by Your Loving
from toes
to fingertips,
as every hair
upon our heads
and skin
tells us
stories
of Your nearness,
O Most Gracious One.
You who have no limit
in Your Loving,
expand ours,
that we might extend
ourselves

to include
each other
in the precious,
most precious
secret
held
within these hearts—
You surround us
with Your Knowing
and would have us know
that Your Word
is always
on the tip of our tongues,
waiting to be heard—
let us speak
the words of healing
and offer greetings of peace
from the depths
of our souls
to everyone around us,
and to those
who came before,
rectifying the balance
that may have
gone off kilter
and providing
ways of rectitude
for future
generations—
these children
of our hearts
who have yet to be,
and intertwine
us all,
for all eternity.
Ya Samad,

Ya Mumin,
Ya Muhaymin,
Ya Warith,
O You Who Are Eternal,
Satisfier of All Needs,
You Who Are Most Faithful,
Who Inspire Our Faith,
You in Whose Embrace We Are Secure,
O Best Inheritor of All.

Ya Warith, O Best Inheritor of All,
Al Khaliq, The Creator, *Al Bari*, The Patterner,
Al Musawwir, The Shaper of Form,
Al Wadud, The Infinitely Loving One, *Al 'Alim*, The All Knowing,
Ya Samad, O You Who Are Eternal, Satisfier of All Needs,
Ya Mumin, O You Who Are Most Faithful, Inspirer of Faith,
Ya Muhaymin, O You in Whose Embrace We Are Secure

O human being! Truly, you are laboring towards your Sustainer,
painfully struggling, but then you shall meet Him/Her.
[84:6]

He/She is the One who causes the dawn to break;
and He/She has made the night to be a source of stillness,
and the sun and the moon for reckoning
by the order of the Almighty, the All Knowing.
And He/She it is who has made the stars for you
so that you might be guided by them
through the darknesses of land and sea:
clearly have We detailed Our signs for people of inner knowing.
And He/She it is who has brought you all into being
out of a single soul,
and so designated for each of you a time-limit on earth
and a resting-place after death:
clearly have We detailed Our signs for people who can grasp the truth.
[6:96–98]

Say: "O my Sustainer! Cause me to reach a blessed alighting—
for You are the best to show the human being how to reach his alighting!"
[23:29]

And indeed, We have set up in the heavens great constellations,
and endowed them with beauty for all to behold.
[15:16]

And God sets forth as an example to those who have faith
the wife of Pharaoh:
witness, she said: "O my Sustainer!
Build for me in nearness to You a mansion in the Garden
and save me from Pharaoh and his actions
and save me from those who do wrong."
[66:11]

O my servants who have faith!
truly, My earth is spacious,
so serve Me alone!
Every soul shall have a taste of death:
in the end to Us shall you all be brought back.
But those who have faith and do good deeds,
to them shall We give a home in the Garden—
lofty mansions beneath which rivers flow—
to dwell there always,
an excellent reward for those who act rightly—
those who persevere in patience
and put their trust in their Sustainer.
[29:56–59]

Say: "The Truth is from your Lord . . ."
As for those who have faith and do the deeds of wholeness and reconciliation,
truly, We shall not allow to perish
the recompense of anyone who does a good deed.
[18:29–30]

To Him/Her belongs what is in the heavens and on earth
and all between them and all beneath the soil.
Whether you pronounce the word aloud or not,
truly, He/She knows what is secret and what is yet more hidden.
God! there is no god but Hu!
To Him/Her belong the Most Beautiful Names.
[20:6–8]

And there is not a thing but its storehouses are with Us;
but We only send it down in appropriate measures.
And We send the fertilizing winds,
then cause the rain to descend from the sky
and so provide you with water
though you are not the guardians of its stores.
And, truly, it is We who give life and who give death:
it is We who are the Inheritor and Sustainer of All.
And well do We know those who lived before you
and those who will come after you.
Surely, it is your Sustainer who will gather them all together.
Truly, He/She is All Wise, All Knowing.
[15:21–25]

98. Ar Rashid, The Righteous Teacher

Ya Rashid, Ya Nafi, Ya Wadud

O Most Gracious Teacher,
we wait upon Your Word,
Your life-giving Word,
You who grant life
and bestow death,
and life again, Everlasting,
Ya Muhyi, Ya Mumit,
Ya Hayy, Ya Qayyum—
continually, You are opening
and closing doors we cannot see;
we cannot turn the handle,
You alone hold the key
to the moments of our passages
from There to here
and here to There,
where You are always with us.
Even here, You never leave us;
why would we think so?
Perhaps we fail to listen
to our own hearts—
these throbbing presences
within our chests
that resonate with You
with every breath,
though we may fail to hear—
tune our ears!
O You who miss no sound
of our awakening
and gently nurse us
at Your breast,
kindest of mothers,

like Moses we accept
only Your sustenance
and turn from any other nurse,
resting in Your arms,
we recognize that taste—
such sweetness,
true Mother's milk,
how could we want anything else?
Ya Muqit, O You who provide
the best of sustenance!
Listening,
listening,
turning within,
and without,
to bring the depths
to Light
and Light
to the depths of recognition,
everywhere we see Your Face.
Ya Sami, Ya Basir, Ya Wadud,
O You who are All Hearing,
the All Seeing, the Most Loving,
the moments You have given us,
let us not waste them,
but truly turn them into goodness.
Ya Nafi, O You
who are the Creator of All Goodness,
share Your skill
with these hearts
who are dependent upon You
and would be interwoven
by that Rightfulness.
Teach us, O Best of Teachers, Ya Rashid!

Ya Rashid, O Most Righteous Teacher,
Ya Muhyi, O You Who Bestow Life, *Ya Mumit*, O You Who Bestow Death,
Ya Hayy, O Ever Living One, *Ya Qayyum*, O Self-Subsisting, Eternal One,
Ya Muqit, O You Who Provide the Best of Sustenance,
Ya Sami, O You Who Are All Hearing, *Ya Basir*, O All Seeing One,
Ya Wadud, O Infinitely Loving One,
Ya Nafi, O You Who Are the Creator of All Goodness

In truth, it is up to Us to guide,
and truly, to Us belong the End and the Beginning.
[92:12–13]

Let there be no compulsion in matters of faith,
surely rightfulness stands clearly apart from error,
and the one who turns away from all harmfulness
and has faith in the Divine Reality
has surely grasped the most trustworthy handhold which shall never give way.
And God is All Hearing, All Knowing.
[2:256]

And so, I spread My Own love over you [O Moses] —
in order that you might be formed under My eye:
When your sister went forth and said [to Pharaoh's people],
"Shall I guide you to one who might nurse and rear him?"
And so We returned you to your mother,
so that her eye might be gladdened, and that she might not sorrow . . . .
I have chosen you for My Own service.
Go forth, you and your brother, with My messages,
and never tire of remembering Me.
[20:39–42]

Wherever you turn, there is the Face of God.
Witness, God is Infinite, All Knowing.
[2:115]

I call to witness this land
in which you are free to dwell,
and the bond between parent and child:
truly, We have created the human being to labor and struggle.
Does he or she think that no one has power over him or her?
He/she may boast: "I have spent abundant wealth!"
Does he think that no one sees him?
Haven't We made a pair of eyes for him?
And a tongue and a pair of lips?
And shown him the two ways?
But he has not quickened along the path that is steep.
And what will explain to you what the steep path is?—
the freeing of one who is enslaved,
or the giving of food in time of need
to the orphan with claims of relationship,
or to the helpless, lowly one in the dust,
and being of those who have faith and encourage patience,
and who encourage deeds of kindness and compassion.
These are the companions of blessed righteousness.
[90:1–18]

99. As Sabur, The Most Patient

Ya Sabur, Ya Hamid, Ya Salaam, Ya Haqq, Ya Wadud

It is a golden time
when Your Sabr
is shining.
We wait,
knowing time
is passing,
patient
with the Decree
of God,
and yet yearning . . .
You bring us
through
a tunnel of Love,
when first we are birthed,
and in this life of longing
we traverse
mountains
and pass through
hidden passages
among the rocks,
treacherous turnings,
and open plains,
upon whose lap
we can see the sky
and rest awhile
among Your Stars.
Long journeys,
and sometimes short—
You guard us;
from Your Beneficence
we learn to trust

in Your Munificence
and the beam of Love
that pulls us
ever nearer
to our Home—
the abode where angels
welcome travelers
through every gate
of the City of Love.
For those who patiently persevere—
for them is forgiveness
and a great reward—
the Garden
where birds of grace
are always singing,
praising You,
and radiating
greetings
of Peace,
amid the Greenness
that renews and restores
while the dust of the journey
is washed away
with clean water
from sparkling springs,
and we can see that You
and the Garden
have always been with us,
for *God is with*
those who patiently
persevere,
who gift again
the graces
given,
and bow their heads
in prayer.

You alone
do we ask for help,
You who Love to love,
and restore
all things
to Truth.
Ya Haqq,
Ya Wali,
Ya Wadud.

Ya Sabur, O Most Patient, Inspirer of Patience,
Ya Hamid, O Most Praiseworthy,
Ya Salaam, O You Who Are Peace,
Ya Haqq, O Truth,
Ya Wali, O Friend and Protector,
Ya Wadud, O Infinitely Loving One

O you who have attained to faith!
Seek help through steadfast patience and prayer:
for see how God is with those who patiently persevere.
[2:153]

To bear yourselves with patience
is indeed far better for those who are patient in adversity.
So endure with patience, always remembering that your patience is from God . . .
For, truly, God is with those who are conscious of Him/Her
and are doers of the good.
[16:126–128]

Upon those will be garments of green silk and brocade;
and they will be adorned with bracelets of silver.
And their Sustainer will give them to drink of a drink most pure.
"Truly, all this is your recompense,
since your endeavor has met with Goodly acceptance!"
[76:21–22]

Those who patiently persevere and do good deeds;
for them is forgiveness and a great reward.
[11:11]

In the Name of God, the Infinitely Compassionate and Infinitely Merciful:
Consider time . . .
Truly, human beings are in loss
except those who have faith and do righteous deeds
and encourage each other in the teaching of Truth
and of patient perseverance.
[103:1–3 complete]

"Patience is the key to joy."
[~ Mevlana Jalaluddin Rumi, *Mathnawi* I: 2908]

"Patience is the key to success.
The remedy of patience will burn away the veils over your eye
and open your heart.
When the mirror of your heart becomes clear and pure,
you will behold sights beyond this world of water and earth.
You will behold both the image and the Image-Maker,
both the carpet of the spiritual dominion
and the One Who Spreads It."
[~ Mevlana Jalaluddin Rumi, *Mathnawi* II:70–73]

Only they who are endowed with insight keep this in mind,
those who are true to their bond with God
and do not break their covenant;
those who keep together what God has commanded to be joined,
and stand in awe of their Sustainer and the awesome reckoning to come;
those who patiently persevere seeking the Face of their Sustainer,
and are constant in prayer, who distribute secretly and openly
from what We have given them for their sustenance,
and turn away evil with good:
for these is the fulfillment of the ultimate Abode—
gardens of endless bliss—which they shall enter
together with the righteous among their parents,

their spouses, and their offspring,
and angels shall greet them from every gate:
"Peace be with you for having patiently persevered!
Then how excellent is the final dwelling-place!"
[13:19–24]

Index

A

Abraham 23, 44, 56, 57, 63, 71, 96, 174, 213, 214, 221, 242, 262, 266, 269

Abundance 31, 39, 41, 91, 92, 100, 135, 150, 186, 191, 211, 214, 235, 238, 242

Adam 27, 53, 95, 110, 221, 233, 274

Al 'Adl, The Most Just 73–76; also 134–36, 180–83, 206–9, 236–39

Al 'Afuw, The One Who Forgives and Erases the Traces 29–32

Al Ahad, The One, All Inclusive In Your Unity 199–202; also 66–68, 137–140, 154–56, 166–71

Al Akhir, The Last 215–17; also 25–28

Al 'Ali, The Most High 94–97; also 223–26

Al 'Alim, The All Knowing 48–50; also 15–18, 41–44, 45–47, 58–61, 66–68, 83–86, 98–100, 107–110, 111–15, 130–33, 223–26, 278–83

Angels 12, 15, 16, 41, 60, 61, 63, 64, 88, 89, 106, 128, 129, 134, 136, 138, 172, 174, 177, 188, 194, 195, 202, 207, 209, 213, 224, 226, 233, 246, 249, 250, 252, 253, 256, 257, 258, 289, 292

Attention 53, 79, 117, 268, 274

Al Awwal, The First 215–17; also 25–28

Al 'Azim, The Most Magnificent 87–90; also 94–97

Al 'Aziz, The Almighty, Most Dear 19–21; also 87–90, 161–63

B

Al Badi, The Skilful Original Creator 272–74; also 19–21, 161–63, 176–79

Al Ba'ith, The Resurrector 144–46; also 137–40, 176–179

Al Baqi, The Truly Abiding One 275–77; also 101-6, 137–40, 144–46, 176–79

Al Bari, The Evolver, The Patterner 25–28; also 215–17, 278–83

Al Barr, The Bestower of Beneficence 227–232

Al Basir, The All Seeing 66–68; also 11–14, 41–44, 62–65, 77–80, 98–¬100, 107–10, 111–15, 259–262, 284–87

Al Basit, The Expander 51–54

Al Batin, The Hidden 218–22; also 151–53

Beauty ix, xi, xiv, 21, 26, 27, 28, 41, 58, 69, 74, 84, 109, 110, 116, 124, 138, 215, 223, 248, 250, 264, 273, 274, 282

Beautiful ix, xi, xiii, xv, 3, 23, 25, 26, 27, 28, 35, 56, 63, 70, 76, 100, 101, 115, 117, 130, 146, 150, 175, 181, 190, 199, 201, 206, 209, 215, 221, 247, 250, 261, 276, 277, 283

Bible x, 14, 65, 71, 79, 121, 139, 140, 171, 238, 250, 258

Birth 12, 80, 81, 126, 223, 259, 288

Book x, xv, 39, 64, 68, 69, 70, 92, 96, 100, 105, 135, 165, 166, 170, 204, 237, 257, 261, 270

Burden 53, 72, 88, 96, 114, 127, 128, 260

C

Charity 17, 53, 85, 150, 156, 159, 193, 214, 261

Children 27, 29, 38, 53, 64, 68, 95, 102, 108, 110, 155, 221, 236, 238,

240, 241, 250, 274, 275, 280
Cup, Goblet 228, 231, 258

D

Ad Darr, The Creator of the Harmful, The Afflicter 227–32
Day xi, xiii, 1, 3, 4, 16, 32, 35, 39, 46, 48, 55, 67, 71, 83, 85, 87, 112, 145, 147, 156, 161, 165, 167, 170, 172, 174, 180, 182, 188, 189, 191, 193, 195, 197, 215, 224, 244, 246, 250, 253, 258, 263, 266
Day of Alast 95, 96, 253
Day of Reckoning 13, 27, 46, 60, 73, 75, 89, 114, 118, 128, 139, 141, 146, 174, 178, 193, 208, 209, 243, 257
Death 13, 96, 115, 125, 160, 185, 186, 187, 239, 254, 281, 282, 283, 284, 286
Desire 73, 98, 121, 127, 128, 149, 191, 233, 245, 252, 272
Despair 7, 144, 237, 254, 268
Devotion 44, 75, 139, 156
Difficulty 53, 214
Doubt 133, 257, 268

E

East 4, 17, 81, 82, 128, 156, 166, 170, 238, 256, 265
Essence 23, 95, 135, 178, 199

F

Face xv, 14, 16, 17, 34, 49, 55, 59, 66, 68, 71, 74, 76, 94, 103, 104, 106, 112, 114, 117, 118, 119, 125, 128, 141, 152, 170, 190, 192, 203, 210, 216, 217, 219, 251, 266, 285, 286, 291
Fasting 17, 126
Father xiv, 57, 214
Al Fattah, The Opener: 45–47; also 37–40, 48–50, 141–143

Fear 8, 10, 32, 49, 75, 81, 180, 183, 190, 225, 249, 257, 258
Felicity 112, 114, 119, 165, 183, 228, 231
Fire 82, 91, 149, 180, 236, 265, 269
St. Francis of Assisi x, xiv, xv

G

Garden x, 9, 13, 14, 17, 20, 21, 36, 44, 53, 61, 65, 70, 71, 72, 73, 75, 76, 90, 115, 121, 126, 136, 138, 139, 145, 146, 148, 150, 158, 160, 170, 172, 175, 178, 182, 183, 190, 191, 194, 214, 228, 231, 241, 247, 249, 255, 257, 267, 274, 277, 282, 289, 291
Al Ghaffar, The One Who Loves to Forgive 29–32
Al Ghafur, The Oft Forgiving 29–32; also 83–86, 195–98
Al Ghani, The One Who Is Rich, Without Need 259–62; also 166–71
Grace 4, 30, 33, 34, 38, 40, 41, 52, 57, 66, 79, 91, 98, 101, 104, 111, 141, 143, 146, 153, 156, 161, 167, 178, 180, 186, 188, 189, 195, 206, 207, 227, 228, 229, 230, 241, 242, 245, 247, 261, 278, 289
Gratitude x, xi, 39, 50, 52, 79, 85, 91, 92, 93, 112, 113, 169, 189, 225, 239, 254, 260, 266

H

Al Hadi, The Guide 268–71; also 8–10, 19–21, 73–76, 101–6
Hadith 28, 54, 57, 67, 71, 218, 226, 258
Hadith Qudsi ix, 7, 44, 54, 61, 159, 194, 220
Al Hafiz, The Preserver 101–6; also 154–56, 164–65, 180–83
Al Hakam, The Judge 69–72; also 73–76

Al Hakim, The Most Wise, Healer of All Our Ills 134–36; also 19–21, 22–24, 41–44, 87–90

Al Halim, The Most Forbearing 83–86

Al Hamid, The One Worthy of All Praise 166–71; also 101–6, 288–92

Al Haqq, The Truth 151–53; also 8–10, 29–32, 33–36, 66–68, 94–96, 101–6, 107–10, 147–50, 166–71, 210–14, 252–55, 268–71, 288–92

Al Hasib, The Reckoner 111–15

Al Hayy, The Ever Living 188–91; also 4–7, 154–56, 166–71, 227–32, 284–87

Home xv, 13, 19, 22, 56, 82, 88, 113, 115, 144, 145, 147, 155, 177, 184, 203, 210, 213, 234, 245, 252, 275, 282, 289

Hope xiv, 82, 92, 186, 193, 209, 225, 268, 270

Horizon x, 16, 132, 152, 153, 192, 219, 221

Hud 235

Human Being x, 6, 7, 20, 23, 30, 31, 44, 56, 67, 70, 74, 82, 89, 96, 98, 101, 109, 110, 114, 116, 124, 125, 129, 149, 151, 152, 153, 163, 174, 178, 182, 183, 185, 193, 204, 208, 213, 214, 218, 225, 226, 237, 238, 242, 243, 247, 257, 262, 265, 274, 277, 281, 282, 287, 291

Humility xiv, 17, 49, 58, 59, 60, 101, 190, 201

I

Isaac 57

Ishmael 57, 63, 174, 262

J

Al Jabbar, The Compeller 22 –24

Jacob 57

Al Jalil, The Mightily Majestic 116–18

Al Jami, The Gatherer 256–58; also 25–29

Jonah 57, 195, 196, 197, 218

Joseph 57, 127, 128, 177

Journey xiv, 16, 50, 76, 77, 221, 257, 288, 289

Jesus 21, 57, 64, 102, 119, 195, 197, 221

K

Kaaba 174, 262

Al Kabir, The Most Great 98–100

Al Karim, The Infinitely Generous One 119–22; also xii, 41–44, 55–57, 83–86, 91–93, 111–15, 123–25, 141–43, 147–50, 154–56, 157–60, 184–87, 192–94, 199–202, 210–14, 218–22, 240–43, 275–77

Al Khabir, The All Aware 80–82; also 11–14, 77–79, 107–10

Al Khafid, The One Who Brings Low 55–57

Al Khaliq, The Creator 25–28; also 157–60, 215–17, 278–83

Knowledge 1, 2, 6, 19, 28, 48, 49, 50, 64, 82, 92, 97, 106, 132, 134, 136, 145, 153, 173, 174, 177, 190, 215, 225, 230, 253, 265

L

Al Latif, The Infinitely Subtle 77–79; also 80–82, 94–97, 172–75

Light xii, xiii, 13, 21, 32, 37, 52, 55, 60, 62, 66, 67, 69, 70, 71, 74, 78, 79, 80, 81, 82, 89, 91, 95, 96, 104, 109, 127, 135, 138, 141, 147, 151, 161, 162, 164, 172, 180, 184, 192, 195, 196, 200, 207, 217, 223, 224, 228, 231, 241, 242, 246, 252, 258, 263, 264, 265, 266, 269, 278, 279, 285

Lightning 225

Luqman 79, 93

M

Al Majeed, The Sublimely Majestic 141–43
Al Majid, The Magnificent, Tremendous in Glory 195–98; also 166–71
Al Malik ul Mulk, The Sovereign of the Dominion 244–47; also 227–32
Al Malik, The Sovereign 4–7
Al Mani, The Protector from Harm 227–32
Mary 3, 21, 44, 64, 102, 197
Al Matin, The One Who Is Ever Steadfast, Everlastingly Strong 161–63; also 157–60
Men x, 5, 17, 37, 71, 90, 115, 121, 124, 139, 158, 162, 200, 201, 250, 260, 266, 276
Messenger xi, 16, 32, 53, 61, 72, 100, 104, 114, 118, 122, 135, 149, 150, 163, 173, 185, 209, 214, 220, 222, 231, 245, 249, 254, 273
Moon xvi, 35, 57, 60, 62, 71, 109, 167, 170, 174, 223, 224, 246, 264, 266, 281
Moses 32, 57, 64, 68, 96, 102, 105, 127, 128, 142, 221, 238, 246, 285, 286
Mother 85, 126, 225, 284, 285, 286
Mountain 33, 34, 35, 43, 105, 149, 161, 162, 191, 195, 207, 219, 220, 224, 225, 230, 233, 247, 274, 288
Al Mu'akhkhir, The Delayer 210–14
Al Mubdi, The Originator Who Creates Out of Nothing 176–79
Al Mudhill, The One Who Humbles 50–61
Al Mughni, The Enricher 259–62; also 166–71
Muhammad ix, xi, xiii, 2, 7, 12, 16, 28, 32, 43, 54, 57, 67, 71, 94, 100, 103, 104, 122, 135, 149, 185, 207, 209, 214, 218, 220, 226, 236, 237, 245, 249, 258
Al Muhaymin, The Guardian of Security 15–18; also 11–14, 278–83
Al Muhsi, The One Who Keeps Account 172–75
Al Muhyi, The One Who Gives Life 184–87; also 284–87
Al Mu'id, The Restorer 180–83; also 41–44, 83–86, 111–15, 137–40
Al Mu'izz, The One Who Bestows Honor 58–61
Al Mujib, The One Who Responds 126–29; also 123–25
Al Mumin, The Most Faithful, The Inspirer of Faith 15–18; also 11–14, 111–15, 252–55, 278–83
Al Mumit, The One Who Takes Life 184–87; also 284–87
Al Muntaqim, The Rectifier 236–39
Al Muqaddim, The Expediter 210–214
Al Muqit, The Nourisher 107–10; also 37–40, 41–44, 172–75, 284–87
Al Muqsit, The One Who Keeps the Balance, The Equitable 252–55; also 41–44, 111–15, 180–83
Al Muqtadir, The Determiner 206–9
Al Musawwir, The Shaper of Form 25–28
Al Muta'ali, The Supremely High 223–226; also 94–97
Al Mutakabbir, The Supremely Great 22–24; also 98–100

N

An Nafi, The Creator of All Good 227–32; also 284–87
Night xi, xvi, 3, 13, 32, 35, 46, 55, 57, 64, 67, 71, 83, 85, 100, 105, 132, 134, 145, 147, 155, 156, 160, 163, 165, 167, 170, 172, 174, 188, 189, 193, 197, 207, 209, 217, 220, 224, 246, 253, 263, 264, 265, 266, 270, 279, 281

Noah 32, 57, 221
An Nur, The Light 263–67; also xii, xiii, 66–68, 69–72, 77–79, 80–82, 94–97, 107–10, 137–140, 164–65, 195–98, 240–43

P

Path 2, 6, 15, 45, 60, 66, 72, 77, 88, 95, 109, 120, 149, 165, 167, 174, 178, 221, 246, 258, 268, 270, 271, 274, 276, 287
Poverty 148, 243
Prayer xi, xiii, xiv, xv, 17, 43, 53, 79, 92, 94, 100, 104, 115, 123, 124, 129, 150, 155, 156, 159, 163, 174, 177, 186, 193, 202, 214, 216, 219, 242, 257, 261, 262, 270, 276, 289, 290, 291
Presence 11, 12, 19, 23, 32, 52, 55, 56, 78, 91, 94, 97, 101, 102, 107, 110, 113, 115, 132, 137, 139, 148, 161, 171, 183, 188, 195, 199, 200, 203, 204, 209, 218, 220, 255, 258, 261, 263, 270, 284
Pride 206
Prophet ix, xi, xiii, 2, 7, 12, 28, 43, 44, 52, 54, 56, 57, 67, 71, 79, 93, 94, 100, 119, 128, 143, 150, 151, 177, 208, 209, 226, 246, 258
Prostration 13, 55, 88, 94, 104, 142, 174, 204, 213

Q

Al Qabid, The Constrictor 51–54
Al Qadir, The Pourer of Power 206–9; also 107–110, 172–75
Al Qahhar, The Overwhelming, Irresistible 33–36; also 37–40
Al Qawi, The Source of All Power 157–60; also 272–74
Al Qayyum, The Eternal, Self-Subsisting Source 188–91; also 227–32, 284–87

Al Quddus, The Most Holy and Pure 8–10; also 4–7, 33–36, 77–79, 107–10, 137–40, 144–46, 147–50, 154–56, 199–202
Quran ix, x, xi, xv, 3, 7, 43, 49, 79, 81, 103, 109, 155, 209, 225, 261, 262, 269, 270

R

Ar Rafi, The Exalter 55–57
Ar Rahim, The Infinitely Merciful 1–3; also 4–7, 37–40, 69–72, 80–82, 94–97, 98–100, 107–10, 141–43, 147–50, 166–71, 195–98, 210–14, 240–43, 248–51
Ar Rahman, The Infinitely Compassionate 1–3; also 4–7, 48–50, 87–90, 98–100, 107–110, 141–43, 184–87, 188–91, 210–14, 240–43, 248–51, 272–74
Rain 1, 2, 33, 82, 117, 126, 146, 186, 188, 189, 192, 223, 226, 247, 283
Ar Raqib, The Ever Watchful One 123–25; also 126–29, 154–56, 203–5
Ar Rashid, The Most Righteous Teacher 284–87
Ar Rauf, The Most Kind 240–43; also 48–50, 83–86, 141–43, 184–87, 218–222
Ar Razzaq, The Provider 41–44; also 107–10, 195–98
Remembrance ix, xi, 1, 9, 13, 17, 20, 29, 30, 31, 49, 53, 60, 64, 79, 82, 91, 92, 96, 99, 100, 101, 127, 129, 139, 146, 148, 156, 165, 168, 176, 177, 193, 196, 204, 205, 209, 211, 233, 238, 239, 241, 246, 247, 250, 251, 256, 257, 258, 261, 275, 276, 286, 290
Repentance 2, 9, 31, 63, 129, 230, 233, 234, 235, 255, 276
Resurrection 46, 75, 103, 112, 138,

144, 145, 172, 177, 178, 201, 229, 247
Righteousness 3, 9, 44, 57, 72, 76, 100, 114, 121, 135, 140, 146, 150, 152, 160, 165, 177, 178, 194, 201, 208, 214, 216, 226, 234, 238, 250, 258, 260, 262, 269, 276, 277, 284, 285, 286, 287, 291
Rumi x, xi, xiii, 93, 108, 110, 119, 151, 218, 291

S

As Sabur, The Most Patient, Inspirer of Patience 288–92; also 83–86
As Salaam, The One Who Is Peace 11–14; also 41–44, 69–72, 73–76, 83–86, 98–100, 144–46, 161–63, 180–83, 203–5, 240–43, 275–77, 288–92
Salih 129, 235, 273
As Samad, The Eternal, Satisfier of All Need 203–5; also 11–14, 101–6, 164–65, 199–202, 210–14, 240–43, 278–83
As Sami, The All Hearing 62–65; also xvi, 11–14, 41–44, 77–79, 107–10, 199–202, 259–62, 284–87
Sea 4, 11, 39, 57, 77, 79, 102, 108, 119, 121,124, 126, 158, 178, 191, 203, 218, 219, 221, 223, 233, 253, 266, 278, 281
Seek, search x, xiii, 32, 39, 41, 66, 68, 95, 101, 104, 113, 114, 119, 126, 128, 157, 168, 182, 189, 192, 203, 207, 231, 234, 243, 244, 261, 271, 290, 291
Servant 9, 13, 27, 35, 43, 44, 50, 54, 57, 64, 82, 92, 94, 125, 186, 190, 191, 193, 226, 230, 231, 242, 244, 254, 259, 282
Ash Shahid, The Witness 147–50; also 25–28, 111–15, 123–25
Ash Shakur, The Grateful, Ever Responsive to Gratitude 91–93; also 51–54, 111–15
Shams of Tabriz 108, 110, 151, 218
Shu'ayb 31, 128, 208
Solomon 57, 65, 137, 139, 140, 143, 262
Soul ix, 12, 13, 14, 15, 31, 36, 68, 71, 72, 91, 93, 105, 124, 151, 156, 174, 199, 201, 206, 208, 211, 238, 249, 250, 258, 259, 260, 261, 280, 281, 282
Spirit x, xv, 8, 74, 94, 96, 108, 119, 211, 291
Spring 17, 80, 142, 160, 170, 177, 181, 210, 228, 231, 247, 268, 274, 289
Star 55, 57, 58, 66, 82, 95, 96, 98, 100, 101, 105, 107, 130, 131, 132, 141, 142, 154, 156, 162, 172, 174, 195, 219, 220, 223, 244, 264, 265, 266, 268, 278, 281, 288
Sun 1, 2, 31, 33, 35, 57, 60, 66, 71, 77, 81, 87, 108, 109, 110, 123, 141, 151, 158, 161, 163, 167, 170, 174, 191, 192, 210, 218, 223, 224, 246, 258, 263, 264, 266, 281
Surrender 10, 17, 63, 71, 136, 149, 177, 183, 201, 214, 230, 239, 250, 254, 270, 271

T

At Tawwab, The One Who Turns Us in Repentance 233–35
Throne 2, 3, 28, 61, 88, 89, 95, 97, 132, 144, 145, 160, 179, 216, 220, 224, 231, 250, 256
Treasure ix, 5, 7, 45, 59, 61, 99, 159, 192, 194, 207, 220, 248, 253
Trust xi, 12, 13, 15, 17, 18, 57, 64, 76, 89, 96, 105, 106, 127, 128, 190, 209, 215, 245, 273, 282, 286, 288

U

Unity 26, 177, 199, 256
Unseen ix, xv, 5, 7, 9, 39, 48, 51, 61, 139, 159, 163, 194, 220, 253

W

Al Waali, The Guardian, Bestower of Bounty 223–26
Al Wadud, The Infinitely Loving 137–40; also xii, 1–3, 4–7, 8–10, 15–18, 19–21, 22–24, 25–28, 33–36, 37–40, 41–44, 45–47, 48–50, 55–57, 58–61, 77–79, 83–86, 87–90, 91–93, 94–97, 98–100, 101–6, 107–110, 111–15, 116–18, 119–122, 126–29, 130–33, 134–136, 141–43, 144–46, 154–56, 161–63, 166–71, 180–83, 184–87, 188–191, 192–94, 195–98, 199–202, 203–5, 210–14, 218–22, 227–32, 240–43, 248–51, 256–58, 259–62, 263–67, 268–71, 272–74, 278–83, 284–87, 288–92
Al Wahhab, The Ever Giving One, Who Overcomes All Obstacles 37–40; also 19–21, 91–93, 98–100, 119–22, 154–56, 272–74
Al Wahid, The One, The Unique 199–202; also 33–36
Al Wajid, The Finder 192–94; also 98–100, 144–46, 166–71, 203–5, 233–35
Al Wakil, The Guardian of All Affairs 154–56; also 8–10, 25–28, 29–32, 137–40, 180–83
Al Wali, The Friend and Protector 164–65; also 29–32, 137–140, 180–83, 268–71, 288–292
Al Warith, The Inheritor of All 278–83; also 215–17, 25–28, 154–56
Al Wasi, The Infinite, All Encompassing One 130–33; also 37–40, 41–44, 98–100, 107–10, 111–15, 161–63, 263–67

Water 1, 2, 3, 8, 20, 22, 29, 35, 44, 45, 46, 47, 49, 51, 53, 59, 67, 72, 76, 77, 80, 90, 108, 115, 116, 117, 129, 136, 139, 141, 142, 144. 146, 150, 153, 158, 159, 161, 172, 175, 177, 178, 187, 191, 194, 206, 211, 224, 225, 228, 233, 245, 255, 258, 267, 269, 274, 277, 278, 283, 289, 291
Wealth x, 96, 183, 261, 287
Wind 46, 67, 73, 88, 98, 146, 178, 186, 187, 227, 229, 247, 250, 283
Wings 50, 84, 88, 124, 207, 258
Women x, 5, 17, 37, 71, 90, 115, 124, 139, 158, 200, 260, 266, 276
Word xv, 3, 4, 11, 20, 22, 23, 24, 39, 42, 44, 47, 63, 64, 68, 69, 74, 75, 76, 78, 87, 103, 105, 108, 110, 119, 121, 125, 127, 134, 136, 143, 146, 151, 152, 155, 156, 186, 195, 219, 220, 230, 234, 236, 244, 248, 250, 253, 277, 280, 283, 284
Work x, 9, 152, 236, 250
The World ix, xi, xiii, xv, 2, 3, 5, 7, 24, 27, 39, 44, 45, 48, 51, 55, 57, 60, 61, 64, 71, 74, 78, 79, 89, 105, 106, 113, 159, 161, 175, 177, 186, 189, 190, 194, 196, 197, 203, 207, 211, 212, 214, 220, 222, 232, 242, 249, 256, 262, 265, 270, 274, 291

Z

Az Zahir, The Manifest 218–22; also 151–53
Zhul Jalali wal Ikram, The Lord of Power and Abundant Beneficence 248–51

Other Publications by Camille Helminski

Threshold Society: www.sufism.org

Words from the East
Poetic reflections, first in the series of "Songs of the Soul"
Camille Hamilton Adams Helminski

Rumi and His Friends, Stories of the Lovers of God
Excerpts from the *Manaqib al-'Arifin* of Aflaki, Selected and Translated by Camille Adams Helminski with Susan Blaylock

The Rumi Daybook, 365 Poems and Teachings from the Beloved Sufi Master
Selected and Translated by Kabir Helminski and Camille Helminski

Women of Sufism: A Hidden Treasure, Writings and Stories of Mystic Poets, Scholars, and Saints
Selected and Introduced by Camille Helminski

Rumi's Sun: The Teachings of Shams of Tabriz
Translated by Refik Algan and Camille Helminski

The Light of Dawn, Daily Readings from the Holy Qur'an
Selected and Rendered by Camille Helminski

Awakened Dreams, Raji's Journeys with the Mirror Dede
Ahmet Hilmi, Translated by Refik Algan and Camille Helminski

The Pocket Rumi Reader (Shambhala Pocket Classics)
Edited by Kabir Helminski (translations by Kabir and Camille)

Rumi Daylight, A Daybook of Spiritual Guidance—Three Hundred and Sixty-Five Selections from the Mathnawi of Mevlana Jalaluddin Rumi
Translated by Camille and Kabir Helminski

Jewels of Remembrance, A Daybook of Spiritual Guidance from the Wisdom of Mevlana Jalaluddin Rumi
Selected and Translated by Kabir and Camille Helminski

The Book of Nature: A Sourcebook of Spiritual Perspectives on Nature and the Environment
The Book Foundation Education Project Series, Edited by Camille Helminski

The Book of Character: An Anthology of Writings on Virtue from Islamic and Other Sources
The Book Foundation Education Project Series, Edited by Camille Helminski

Happiness without Death, Desert Hymns
Assad Ali, Translated by Camille Adams Helminski, Kabir Helminski, Dr. Ibrahim Al-Shihabi

The Mevlevi Wird: the Prayers Recited Daily by Mevlevi Dervishes (the tradition of Rumi)
Translation of the *Awrad-i Sharif*, Offered by Camille Helminski, with assistance from Cuneyt Erolu, Mahmoud Mostafa, and Amer Latif

RECORDINGS:

Glorious Morning Light (Qur'anic recitation by Camille)
The Mevlevi Wird (English recitation by Camille Helminski; Arabic recitation by Mahmoud Mostafa)
The Teachings of Shams of Tabriz (Excerpts from *Rumi's Sun*)
You Are Joy (Rumi recitations by Kabir and Camille with Sufi music from around the world)
Garden within the Flames (offered on CD Baby)—*ilahis* sung by Kabir and Camille (Dost)

www.ingramcontent.com/pod-product-compliance
Lightning Source LLC
Chambersburg PA
CBHW020416010526
44118CB00010B/280